UNDERSTANDING
the USE of
HANDGUNS
for SELF-DEFENSE

DAVID NASH

43-08 162nd Street
Flushing, NY 11358
www.LooseleafLaw.com
800-647-5547

NOTE: All characters, stories and examples are fictional. The thoughts, feelings, stories, notes and opinions are solely that of the author and not the NYPD, John Jay College or the City of New York. This work should not be taken as legal advice and all investigators are strongly encouraged to follow their department's legal and investigative guidelines.

Library of Congress — Cataloging-in-Publication Data

Nash, David, 1939-
   Understanding the use of handguns for self-defense : what you need to know / David Nash.
       p. cm.
   Includes index.
   ISBN 978-1-60885-025-9
 1. Firearms--Evaluation. 2. Pistols. 3. Self-defense--Equipment and supplies. 4. Shooting. I. Title.
   TS534.5.N37 2011
   683.4--dc22

                                                                    2010047375

Cover by *Sans Serif,* Saline, Michigan

Dedication

"People sleep peaceably in their beds at night only because rough men stand ready to do violence on their behalf."

— George Orwell

This book is dedicated to those brave men who sacrificed everything so that I could have the freedom to author a book like this, and for you to have the freedom to read it.

I would also like to thank my mother who once told me, "Raising a child to think for themselves sometimes means they disagree with you." She has always supported me; even though I think she'd rather I was a lawyer...

Table of Contents

About the Author i

Foreword iii

Introduction v

Chapter 1
Mindset 1

Chapter 2
Legal 13

Chapter 3
Safety 21

Chapter 4
What Happens in a Gunfight 31

Chapter 5
Use of Force 37

Chapter 6
Choosing a Gun 51

Chapter 7
Operating a Handgun 61

Chapter 8
Carrying a Gun 81

Chapter 9
Shooting Techniques 89

Chapter 10
Tactics 107

Chapter 11
Common Myths 113

Chapter 12
Dealing with Criticism 117

Chapter 13
Additional Training 121

Index 127

About the Author

David Nash is a former U.S. Marine Corps noncommissioned officer. He has extensive correctional experience as a supervisor at several Tennessee state prisons. David presently works as an emergency management planner and agency firearms instructor for state government.

David spends his free time as an adjunct criminal justice instructor for a local college. He volunteers as the pistol team coach for his school's law enforcement honor society, where, under his guidance, their team has won multiple awards for firearm skill in the southeastern region. David has personally won the 2009 1st place professional individual and 2010 3rd place professional individual shooting awards at the American Criminal Justice Associations Region 5 conference.

In the area of firearms, David is a Certified by the NRA as a Training Counselor, as well as being certified as a law enforcement firearms instructor through the NRA and Tennessee's Law Enforcement and corrections training academies. He holds firearm instructor ratings with several states, including armed security, and handgun carry for Tennessee. He also holds ratings as a Law Enforcement Defensive Tactics Instructor, Chemical Spray Instructor, and Advanced Baton Instructor.

David owns and manages his own firearm training school in Nashville, TN, where he specializes in training inexperienced shooters in becoming more comfortable around and proficient with firearms.

You can find David on the web at the Shepherd School website: www.tngun.com

Foreword

There are numerous resources for experienced shooters, covering everything from the metallurgy of bullets, tweaking triggers and firing mechanisms, the grammatical interpretations of the Miller case, to such exotica as model-specific disarms for martial artists. Much of it is fascinating, some of it, like the last, is hopefully purely hypothetical.

However, that's not where one should start in this complicated field.

What is much less common is a good overview for the beginner or non-expert, who doesn't need a masters' course, just reliable basics. What do common handguns do, how do they work, what should one look for and how does one train to shoot and carry one?

You have a gun. You have a tool that can be used to threaten, kill or be a paperweight, and it all depends on the user—you. This can be an intimidating moment for a rational person. You now have the means to defend yourself. How do you go about doing so?

In this book, David Nash addresses a variety of important issues, starting with the all important mindset. A firearm is only a tool, and of no use without proper thought and training. What is the legality in your area? When you travel to other areas? What are your ethical and moral responsibilities when carrying a firearm? These are subjects usually not addressed in technical books, but of significant import to the average person seeking to defend themselves.

Likewise, think about safety in use and in storage. Most of us will spend time around children. It's very difficult to keep hands-on control of a firearm 24/7. This brings up storage issues. Then there's fear reaction in an emergency situation, dealing with other people, including, in an emergency police. There's a significant amount of strategy and tactics to learn in this subject. It can easily feel daunting and overwhelming.

Nash addresses the outlines and basics of all of this clearly and in a straightforward fashion. This, to me, is the most important part of the book.

Once past these critical issues—and I always recommend even experienced shooters review them regularly—the nuts and bolts of actually choosing, handling and operating a gun is much easier and more comfortable. What type of gun is right for you? Will this change with the weather and location? How do you tell a good holster from hype? Once the important stuff is internalized, these important issues are much less overwhelming and more comfortable.

Cleaning, maintenance, operation. Each of these get attention, and build on the previous material to help the neophyte have a solid grounding with a handgun. Confidence and technique are the most important aspects of using a weapon, but those are built on knowledge and handling.

With this book, one has the tools to learn and seek further instruction, and to be able to identify the skills and resources one needs, as well as how to recognize common myths before they become problems.

If you're experienced with firearms, enjoy the additional resource. If you are new to our community, welcome. We're glad you're here, and you'll find we're a broad but generally friendly and helpful bunch.

I wish you all good and responsible shooting.

— Michael Z. Williamson, USAF (Ret.)
Editor, *Sharp Pointy Things* Blog
michaelzwilliamson.com/bio.php

Introduction

My Credentials

I am not a policeman, I wasn't a special operations warrior, and I don't compete in national level shooting competitions. What I am is a student of the art and science of firearm usage. I am by no means a self-proclaimed or self-important gun guru. I learn from every class I teach. I like teaching, and I particularly like teaching firearm usage.

That's not to say that I have nothing to offer. I grew up around guns (my Dad was a police officer). I carried a pistol in the Marine Corps. I was a firearm instructor for the Tennessee Department of Correction. I am a Tennessee state certified trainer of armed security guards and licensed by three states to teach handgun permit certification courses. I am a certified NRA training counselor (instructor trainer), and I have run my own shooting school for a number of years. However, beyond all of those paper credentials that look nice on the wall, I am a family man who believes in the safety of my family; because of that, I am one who chooses to be an armed citizen.

Introduction to the Shepherd School Mentality

I chose Shepherd School Inc. as the name of my company because I believe that there are human wolves in the world, and someone has to stand to protect the weak. I choose the role of shepherd because I love the sheep. This ideal is not new, as the Bible uses this analogy several times. I cannot hope to do as good a job of explaining the concept as the Bible does; however, Lt. Colonel Dave Grossman, Retired West Point Instructor and U.S. Army psychologist, has written a book called *On Combat*. His book has an outstanding explanation of the ideal of the shepherd and the sheep. It is because of this thinking that I chose Shepherd School and the following motto for my company :

In a World of Wolves, Don't Be a Sheep

Why Another Gun Book?

That being said, you are probably asking, why another gun book? It's not like there aren't enough people selling books, magazines, videos, or courses on shooting, and the Internet is busting at the seams with websites devoted to the gun.

I have noticed that too many times ego gets in the way of instruction. Some men are born with the idea that they can automatically drive fast, make women happy, and shoot a gun just based on their gender. Say one of those men decides that he can shoot a little better than most and later learns he can make decent money teaching firearm use. It could be very easy for him to get sidetracked into believing he is somewhat better than others.

Maybe that doesn't happen to the instructor; maybe it is his students that attribute greatness to him because of their fascination with his personality. No matter the reason, sometimes the teacher's knowledge becomes less of a guide and more of a commandment. This doesn't always happen, but it happens enough that entire cliques are formed based more on the loose talk of a gun writer and less on what actually works for the student.

This book is written from the perspective that it is successful only if it cuts through that personality cult and helps you make your own informed choices. This book is not going to say this gun is better or that gun is worse, or this skill will save you and that one will get you killed. It provides honest information about each side and lets you choose for yourself.

Not everyone likes (or loves) guns or what they stand for. Some are even downright afraid of them. I understand this, even though, by my own admission, it took me some time to understand that not everyone can (or wants to) identify guns used in an action movie based on a ¼-second glimpse. It is okay to have a neutral feeling on firearms; it is also okay to be uncomfortable with violence.

Hopefully, this book will show you that firearms are only tools that someone uses to change his or her situation. My goal is to write for those uncomfortable with guns. I want to state that it is not the tool but the manner of its use that causes problems.

If a school resource officer defends a local school against a madman actively murdering children, it is not the gun that is the hero. It is the policeman. The policeman's actions are not even in the same universe as the madman's. The murderer is evil, not his tools. Does anyone attribute evil to the car that the killer drove to his crime, or the mask he wore? Is the government banning shoes because almost every single bank robber was wearing shoes when he or she robbed a bank?

What I want from this book is for you to come away with the feeling that you can safely and successfully use a firearm if you decide to do so.

How This Book Is Different

Most gun primers are written with an emphasis on shooting. Any legal or psychological information is placed after the fun stuff. This book takes the opposite approach. It starts with the mindset needed to use a firearm in defense of your life, progresses to dealing with other self-defense issues such as what happens in a gunfight, talks about the laws and responsibilities entailed with owning or using a firearm, has an in-depth discussion on safety, moves into the process of choosing a firearm and other tools, and ends with how to actually shoot a handgun.

I also plan for this book to be different in the way the information is passed on to the reader. Most books on this subject either take for granted that the reader has at least some knowledge of firearm use, or are written at such a basic level that they tend to insult the intelligence of the reader. It is my goal to inform, entertain, and, in some small way, reduce the misinformation on firearm usage in America. The colloquial writing style is intentional. I read way too much technical writing where the intended meanings are obscured by the vocabulary and tone. I wrote this just like I would teach it in class.

I hope you enjoy this book as much I enjoyed writing it.

Chapter 1

Mindset

Tactical is an Adjective. Survive is a Verb.
Would you rather Do or Describe?

Preparedness Is Not Paranoia

When we deal with preparedness, we are performing risk assessments. We look into our daily lives and environment, identify threats, categorize them by seriousness, devise methods to deal with those threats, and then take precautions based on balancing the seriousness of the threat with its likelihood. Some examples are: a strike to earth from an asteroid would be devastating, but it's not likely to happen; a paper cut is likely to happen, but it has such minor consequences it does not require preventive measures; but a car crash is serious enough, and likely enough to happen that buying car insurance, or getting a vehicle with air bags, makes sense. Preparing for likely, serious threats is both prudent and responsible.

In this world there are a lot of threats. At any time you could be involved in a car crash, your house may catch on fire, or you could get sick. We as a society understand that these types of problems happen and the responsible person takes precautions to manage these risks. In a world where fire alarms and first aid kits hang on the walls in every public building, we attribute preparation for these situations as a reasonable precaution; but in the same breath, we consider preparing for physical attacks from people paranoia.

What needs to be realized is that although the vast majority of people in this world are normal, well-adjusted, and law-abiding, people, there are criminals who prey on weakness. There is an even smaller subset of criminals that actually enjoy inflicting pain or terror on innocent people. Luckily for us this group is small, but it does not make it unreasonable to identify your likelihood of being attacked and the need to take appropriate preventive measures.

However, that does not mean that it is prudent or reasonable to take preparedness for attack to levels of paranoia. I have known people so ready for a violent attack that they willingly admit to having a plan to kill everyone they speak to if they think the need arises. This level of preparedness is not healthy for the vast majority of the population. Unless you are a secret agent, simply recognizing there is a threat, preparing your reaction to that threat, and then continuing to live your life is much more reasonable.

Most homes have a basic first-aid kit because it is a reasonable, accepted preparedness measure. I doubt you obsess about your kitchen first-aid kit on a daily basis. Owning a firearm is similar. It obviously requires a deeper commitment than buying a first-aid kit. The level of training and practice required far exceeds that for owning a basic first-aid kit, but the idea is the same. Get the equipment if you feel you need it, learn how to use it, and take comfort from knowing that it is one less thing to worry about. If you have a constant nagging feeling about your firearm, you probably unconsciously feel you haven't done enough.

Proper Mindset

Part of the preparation for carrying a handgun for self-defense, or even owning a home protection firearm, is growing a defensive mindset. There are a large number of very good books on this subject. Even though a large amount of money is paid to trainers for helping people develop the proper attitude, you still must do this part yourself. No one can train your mind but you.

You must consider all the ramifications to firearm ownership. Besides parenting, there is no decision you can make that entails the level of responsibility as gun ownership does. When taken with the proper level of seriousness, it is (and should be) a life-changing experience. Deciding within yourself that you are now the master of your destiny, changing from a sheep hoping not to be attacked by the wolves into a shepherd standing firm against attack, is a sobering decision. It involves a serious commitment to an idea of self-determination. You have decided that your right to exist is more important than some cretin's desire for pleasure at your expense.

Awareness

Part of a proper mindset is awareness. It does no good to carry a handgun, have the will and skill to use that handgun, and then be surprised by the thugs lurking just outside the light of an ATM machine. Without awareness, you are still living with the mindset of a victim.

There are two tools used to help you understand situational awareness. Although they both describe the same idea the same way, you rarely hear of them at the same time. These tools are the color code system popularized by the late gun training icon Colonel Jeff Cooper and the National Rifle Association awareness levels as taught in their Personal Protection in the Home curriculum. For purposes of clarity, I have included them both in the following chart.

Color Code	NRA System
White	Unaware
Yellow	Aware
Orange	Alert
Red	Alarm

Figure 1.01
Cooper/NRA Awareness Chart

As your sense of danger increases and you move through the levels of the chart, certain changes take place. This happens because the more your mind becomes ready to fight, the more it prepares your body to fight. We will study this later when we discuss what happens in an actual gunfight. At this time, all you need to know is that the higher the levels of alertness, the less you are able to perform complex tasks or critical thinking. We will go into the reasons for this in Chapter 4.

Condition White/Unaware

You are unaware of what's going on around you. You are not ready. This condition, sadly, is the one most citizens (and all sheep) live in for their entire lives. There are some situations where this is unavoidable. Sleeping, for example, is an activity where it is impossible for you to be in a higher level of awareness. While there

Figure 1.02
Condition White /
Unaware

is no moral connotation of evil attached to this level of awareness, it is not the proper mindset of a person concerned with his or her own safety. Anytime you are outside your home you should strive to not be unaware.

Figure 1.03
Condition Yellow /
Aware

Condition Yellow/Aware

You are alert but calm and relaxed. You are scanning your surroundings for threats. You know who's in front of you, to your sides, and behind you. You are not anticipating an attack, but you are mentally ready in case of one. With practice, you can maintain this level of awareness for extended periods of time. This is the best compromise between readiness and exertion. This is the gold standard of preparedness; try to maintain this level as much as possible.

Condition Orange/Alert

You sense that something is not right, and that you might be attacked. Something has alerted you to danger. Perhaps there are a number of suspicious men standing around your car. Or in the classic Jeff Cooper example, a guy wearing a raincoat comes into your shop on a sweltering summer day. What's wrong with this picture?

Figure 1.04
Condition Orange /
Alert

In the Orange level, you are aware of the positions of all potentially hostile people around you, as well as any weapons they may be able to use, either in their hands or within their reach. You are developing a plan for dealing with the potential hostilities: "... first I take out the guy with the bat, then the big guy near the truck ..." You have also identified multiple escape routes, depending on what response you will use. In addition to being mentally ready, you are physically ready as well.

In the NRA system at this level, you have pre-decided "trigger-points" that cause you to move to the next higher level of awareness. I wholeheartedly endorse this type of thinking. At this level of stress, it is hard to make complex decisions, especially when your decision involves life and death consequences with their respondent legal ramifications. Your decisions deserve and require extensive thought about possible actions you might take to certain stimuli. You most likely will not have the luxury of time to make these decisions in a gunfight if you have not thought seriously about them beforehand.

I run a firearm simulator for a local criminal justice college program; this simulator uses a modified handgun that projects a laser beam on a movie screen. A computer then reads where this laser hits and causes the scenario to change based on the actions of the student. When new students first use the machine, they think it's a high-tech video game but very quickly learn how hard it is to juggle all the parts to a lethal force scenario. Legal justification, tactical considerations, and actual shooting fundamentals come into play. It's not as easy as it looks in the movies. Without a firm understanding of what is and is not justified, as most of the students tend to either freeze or respond to quickly. Luckily, once they have been through a scenario or two, and are able to articulate exactly what justifies lethal force, and how far they are willing to go to protect themselves, they begin to react much more appropriately. The lesson is, just being able to shoot is *not* enough. You must sit down and decide exactly what would cause you to pull your gun in a defensive situation.

Figure 1.05
Condition Red / Alarm

Condition Red/Alarm

The fight is on. You are being actively attacked. There is little time for thinking or second guessing your decisions.

Do What You Need to Do to Survive

The only way to prepare for this is three things: practice, practice, practice. Bruce Lee once said "I fear not the man who has practiced 10,000 kicks once, but I fear the man who has practiced one kick 10,000 times." You have to burn your actions into your muscles so that when the time comes you don't have to think about how to manipulate or *run your gun*.

Remember when you first started driving. It took thought to start the car, to put it in gear, to navigate through town. What would have happened if a dog ran out in front of you your first week of driving? After 10 years or so of driving everyday, has it changed? Do you have to think about starting your car or do you just get in and drive?

If you're going to fight, you do not have time to figure out how to draw or what your sight picture should look like, you need to be in the fight.

Time-Critical Decisions

In the 1950s a young U.S. Air Force fighter pilot named John Boyd—cocky even by fighter-pilot standards—issued a standing challenge to all comers: starting from a position of disadvantage, he'd have his jet on their tail within 40 seconds, or he'd pay out $40. Legend has it that he never lost. His unfailing ability to win any dogfight in 40 seconds or less earned him his nickname, "40-Second" Boyd.

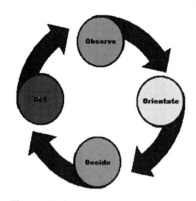

Figure 1.06
OODA Loop Cycle

While undoubtedly this Air Force pilot had a high level of skill with his fighting tool, what made him great was that he knew how to make decisions quickly and accurately under stress. The Air Force was so impressed with his skills they had him create a formal briefing to share this knowledge with other pilots. This short briefing turned into a larger course taught at the Air Force Academy. His system has been partially credited for the outstanding success of American fighter pilots in the Korean War. Colonel Boyd's system is called the OODA loop. OODA is simply an acronym for Observe, Orientate, Decide, and Act.

Observe — A car with engine running parked near your bank, with suspicious looking man in a trench coat loitering near the teller (Yellow).

Orientate — Is this an attempted robbery (upgrade to Orange), or is someone waiting on Granny (stay at Yellow)?

Decide — Does the situation call for force, retreat, or no action? What are you going to do in the situation? How are you going to do this? If you followed my earlier advice and created pre-designated actions based on certain "trigger-points" your response would be made even faster.

Act — Do it! Act decisively and with purpose. Half-steps and lack of follow through cause injury.

The OODA loop explains the mechanism of decision making. The basis of how it applies to self-defense is simple. Once you understand how your attacker makes decisions, you can get inside his OODA and do things that force him to reorient himself so that you can gain a speed advantage. Basically, you want to make your attacker react to you rather than play catch-up to him. Instead of allowing your attacker to act, change the environment to force him to reorient himself. If you are able to do this, it will seem like your attacker is moving in slow motion because you will begin to act while he is reacting to you. This can be easier said than done, but it is an area that deserves attention.

It Takes Longer to React than to Act

The main purpose of awareness is to create a reactionary gap. No matter what level of awareness you start at, when attacked you are going to jump automatically to Alarm/Red. Imagine being awakened to a man on top of you with a knife to your throat. This is a classic example of a condition White to Red response. What being more aware does is to allow you to *recognize* a threat while there is still time to take appropriate action (note, this is not always lethal force; sometimes the appropriate action is leaving the scene, or even submitting). Whatever you action you choose, you will need time to implement it.

Part of reasonable action in a lethal force situation is that your attacker must be able to use deadly force against you right then. While we will discuss this later when we go into the legal aspects of gun ownership, something that will help to reinforce the importance of being aware of your surroundings is knowledge of your reaction time. In law enforcement circles it is commonly taught that the average policeman can draw and fire two rounds center mass in approximately 1.5 seconds. It is also taught that the average attacker armed with an edged weapon (e.g., a knife) can, from a stand still, cross 21 feet and inflict a lethal wound in 1.5 seconds. What this means is that if you are reacting to a threat of this nature, you are going to get hurt. For you to properly respond to threats, you need to be aware of the threat *before* the attack begins.

In our classes we use a rubber knife and a gas-powered, air-soft pistol. I get a student to role-play an armed citizen and arm them with a holster and the airsoft gun. I go across the room with the rubber knife hidden in my pocket. I then ask the student for money, and when they say no (they always say no) I pull my knife and say something like "How 'bout giving me the money now!" Once they say no to me after I have shown the deadly weapon, I run at them with the knife raised. Generally the student gets one shot off but it normally misses me completely (which is good, those bb's hurt). They then get a surprised look and the point is made that …

Distance Equals Time

This drill is called the Tueller drill after a police officer named Dennis Tueller, and it is part of the basis for defense against edged weapon attacks. This is not to say that you should shoot every attacker who wields a knife, but it does illustrate that if you wait until the attacker is about to cut you, it could be too late. You must be aware of your surroundings so that when placed in a situation, you have already orientated yourself to the possible outcomes.

If you have created those mental trigger points, have confidence in your skills, awareness of your surroundings and situation you are way ahead of the game. So much so that in all likelihood any potential criminal can tell you're not an easy target and not put you in the situation to start with.

Could I Shoot Someone?

Being prepared to act violently is not the same as wanting to act violently. Like John Wayne in *The Shootist*, I don't mistreat or insult others and I don't tolerate people treating me that way. Ninety percent of us live by some version of the Golden Rule, but because wolves make up the other 10% of the population, we need to cultivate a defensive mindset. We need to determine in advance if we will use lethal force against someone who is attempting to kill either ourselves or our family. This is not the same as wanting, desiring, or planning to kill.

Figure 1.07
In-class Demonstration of "21 Foot Rule"

Before I allow someone to take my defensive firearm courses, I speak to him or her to get an initial feel of the type of person he or she is. If I get the impression that the prospective student does not have a respect for human life or is not mature enough to handle the responsibility that comes with self-defense firearm ownership, the prospective student will receive a standard, "I am sorry, but our class is full." I will not train someone who wants to kill. I preach avoidance, preparedness, deterrence, and that lethal force is a last resort.

What I do not teach is to regret your actions. Apologies equal guilt. Imagine the following: you are coming home from a late shift at work, rushing to pick up the kids from the baby-sitter. Your spouse is out of town on a business trip. You stop at the ATM to get money to get something for the kids at the drive thru. You notice someone standing near the ATM. He appears to be waiting for someone. He *is* waiting for someone—he is waiting for you. He sees your harried look, your business clothes, your soccer mom car, and your "My Kid Is an Honor Student" sticker. He approaches you, speaks roughly, and produces a knife. Wisely, you gain distance from the attacker by putting the car between him and you. You cannot flee, as the passenger side door is locked, and that's the side you ran to. You try to convince him to leave, but he starts to come around the car. You draw your gun, but he doesn't care. The criminal even makes the statement, "What are you going to do with that?" He starts running toward you. He grabs your arm as you attempt to push him away. He even slices at you with his knife. You have no choice—he forces you to shoot him.

Did you have any other choice in this situation? Did you ask for, desire, or wish for this situation? Was your attacker an innocent person who had no intention of violently killing you? I think you will agree that the answer to these questions is "no." Your response is reasonable, and your actions appropriate. Although I am not remotely suggesting that the act of taking a human life should ever be taken lightly, it is my belief that modern society artificially creates guilt in the minds of citizens who take action to protect their own lives.

Let's put you in a simple scenario. Let us say that a criminal has decided that for whatever reason he wants to graduate to murder today. This criminal goes out and finds a victim, draws his gun, and prepares to kill the innocent. Right before the killer commits his act a police officer appears. What should the officer do? Should he shoot the criminal or let the victim die? Is it moral for the officer to just stand there and let the murderer kill the innocent? If you said no (I hope you said *no*!), explore the feelings behind this.

Why do you feel it is immoral for the police officer to allow the murderer to kill the innocent? Why do you want the cop to shoot the bad guy? Either way someone dies. Why should the person killed be the bad guy? To me it's a simple thing: choice. The only person who chose to commit violence that day was the criminal. The victim sure didn't and the cop would rather end the shift without drawing his weapon.

Let us take away the officer, and make you the innocent. Is it moral for the murderer to kill you? Did you make the decision to seek out a murderer and become a victim? I say to those who say it is never moral to kill that it is never moral to murder. Choosing to allow a criminal to kill you rather than fighting back is saying that the murderer has more of a right to live than you.

We are not police officers, we are civilians. We have no legal duty to protect. If we go out with the intent to kill we become murderers; it does not matter the reason. The above exercise illustrates the moral authority for self-defense. If someone must die, then let it be the person that instigated the situation, not the innocent.

Not everyone has it in them to fight back or to defend themselves with lethal force, and that is okay. However, it is equally okay to defend yourself from attack if able, especially when you are an innocent being attacked by a criminal with a felonious motive. All I ask is that you explore this question in depth, with your spouse and clergy if you have that desire, and honestly decide what would trigger you to use force to defend yourself and then use this knowledge to prepare ways to incorporate self-defense into your lifestyle.

Andy vs. Barney

My mother once said that a lot of today's problems could be solved if school kids watched 30 minutes of *The Andy Griffith Show* each day. I think she's right; there is a lot of good tactical knowledge to be gained from this old show.

How many times has a bad guy laughed at Barney, or has Barney negligently fired into the ground trying to quick draw his pistol? On the other hand, how many times has Sheriff Taylor stopped a crime without even carrying a gun? The difference is mindset. It's based upon confidence. Andy does not need to prove how tough he is, he knows exactly what he can do, so he does not need to prove it at every chance. Barney feels like he gets his authority from his gun, so it's a crutch. A gun is just a piece of iron and wood. It's your mindset that makes the difference. You build that mindset by training and deep contemplation on what you would or wouldn't do to protect you own or your loved one's life.

Chapter 2

Legal

Repercussions of Use of Force

The average cost of defending a justified use-of-force shooting is $40,000. Although I would be willing spend ten times that if it means I get to keep breathing, I will not risk this for pride.

If you are not willing to walk away when someone curses you, insults you in front of your kids, or talks ugly to your wife, think very hard on these repercussions.

I used to teach my officers in the penitentiary that we did not care what a convict said as long as he was doing what he was supposed to do. He could tell us all day long what he was going to do when he "got out," or what he would do when he was "written up." Talk is cheap. I am not willing to trade my freedom for loose talk. More importantly, I am not willing to hurt someone over pride.

You should also be aware that there are people in jail right now who did all the right things in a bad situation. I know a man in prison who took tactically correct action to save his life, but that tactical action did not follow the law. I know a lot more who are incarcerated because they did not have a firm understanding of the law or worse yet had a faulty understanding of it. It is a sobering thought. You must research and decide for yourself if you will risk the repercussions if you wish to exercise your right to carry firearms. Sometimes there is no "right answer."

Carry Laws/Gun Ownership Laws

Laws on the legal ownership and bearing (carrying) of firearms change each year. These laws also change from state to state, or even from town to town. Entire books have been written on the firearm laws of single states. This book is not going to explore carry laws and gun ownership laws in detail; however, this book will discuss some basic concepts.

Some states require registration of each pistol you buy; some even require licenses or place limits on the amount of firearms or types of ammunition you buy. The best place to learn about these rules in most states would be the State Police, Department of Safety, or Bureau of Criminal Investigation. However, this varies; in one state I know of, firearm licensure for both civilian carry and armed security is done through their Department of Agriculture. Each state is different. I would suggest you call your local police department for information on the appropriate regulatory agency so that you can get accurate information.

May Issue

Once you learn how to buy the gun, know that some states do not allow carrying of handguns in any manner. Others have what are known as "may issue" laws. A may issue or discretionary carry law allows the carrying of a firearm with a license; however, the issuing agency, normally the county sheriff, does not have to issue the license. They may deny the application without giving a reason. In places like this, carry permits are often politicized, with some people excluded without recourse. Basically a law like this says the granting authority *may* issue a permit, but they don't have to.

Shall Issue

The next level is known as "shall issue." In shall issue if the applicant meets the state's requirements, the permit must be given to the applicant. Generally the requirements are simple, and they include all or some of the following:

License Fee — Generally between $50.00 and $150.00 for a period of years (normally 4 or 5).
Background Check — The applicant cannot be a felon, addicted to narcotics, mentally disabled, or convicted of or indicted for domestic assault.
Fingerprints
Photograph
Training course — Sometimes this can simply be a certificate from an NRA course. In other states it must be a specific course given by a state licensed instructor.

As a person understands the complexity of firearm training I agree with a requirement that anyone wishing to carry a firearm pass a safety course; however, I also understand the civil liberties involved, and that some people cannot afford course and license fees. The poor have every right to self-protection as the rich. However, it is a balancing act to meet the needs of society as a whole.

Vermont Carry

The greatest freedom to carry is given in states with no laws concerning carrying a firearm. As of today, the only state with no mention of handgun carrying in its laws is Vermont. If you live in Vermont, you may carry a handgun without a license, because there is no law requiring a license.

Alaska has recently changed its laws so that a license is not needed to carry a handgun within the state; however, Alaska does provide a means to get a license so that their residents can carry handguns in other states that allow it.

State Carry Permits Vary from State to State

Differing states also have laws concerning what firearms you may carry and how you may carry them. Kentucky, for instance, has a Concealed Weapon License. A resident with this license may carry almost any weapon as long as it is concealed. Kentucky's law specifically includes blackjacks, saps, and throwing stars. Tennessee has a Handgun Carry Permit. This permit only allows individuals to carry handguns, but you may carry any handgun(s) you want, in any way you like, either in the open or concealed.

Many states recognize other states' licenses. This is normally based on similar requirements. Some states even sign formal reciprocity agreements that specifically recognize other states' permits. For example, a resident of Tennessee with a valid Tennessee Handgun Carry Permit can travel armed in Kentucky.

Figure 2.01

It is important to know that you are bound by the law of the state
you are in and not by the law of the state that issued your license.
An example of this is that a Kentucky permit holder could not use
his or her permit to carry a set of ninja throwing stars when
traveling in Tennessee, nor could a Tennessee permit holder carry
his handgun in the open when in Kentucky.

Some states will give permits to anyone who meets their
requirements, whether they live in the state or not. This is not a
bad thing, as it allows hunters or other travelers access to handguns in that state, even though they may live in a state that may
not allow residents to get permits. Of course, each state's law
applies to their state only. You cannot use an out-of-state permit
to carry a handgun in a way that violates the law of the state you
are in.

For instance, if I lived in New York, I could apply for a Utah
handgun permit, but I could not use it to carry a handgun in New
York because New York does not recognize the Utah permit as
valid. However, if I drove to Tennessee I could carry a handgun in
Tennessee on the Utah permit because Tennessee recognizes it.

Also, you need to be aware that some states choose not to
recognize permits when the license holder is a not a resident of
the issuing state, even if they recognize the same state's permits
when held by a resident. As an example, if while visiting Tennessee from New York, I decided to move to Tennessee, I would have
to get a Tennessee handgun permit, as Tennessee does not allow
residents to carry handguns in state on out-of-state permits.

It seems confusing, but it's not really once you read the actual
laws. The bottom line is that there are many different laws and
rules in each state, and if you choose to carry a gun, it is your
responsibility to know the laws wherever you carry that gun. You
need to consult a lawyer (which I am not) and realize that a state
legislature is free to change a state's law at any time.

Buying a Gun at a Gun Store

Buying a gun as a consumer is normally pretty simple. The
buyer goes to a licensed dealer, chooses his or her firearm, and
fills out a form that asks for identification information. The form
contains questions about felony convictions and background
suitability issues. The dealer will take the buyer's thumbprint
and call the government for an instant background check. As long
as the background check is clear, you may purchase the firearm.

This check should not take longer than 10 minutes or so, but if the check takes longer than three days and you are not denied within that time, you may take possession of the firearm, even if the background check is not ultimately approved.

States are free to make more stringent laws. Some states require a license to buy a gun, or add a waiting period, or even charge additional fees to perform the check. The store where you wish to buy your firearm can describe the specific requirements in your area.

Gun Show Loop-Hole

As a private citizen, you have the right to own property. You also have the right to sell this property. This right also applies to firearms. There is a caveat to the right to sell firearms, however. The U.S. Constitution allows the federal government to regulate interstate commerce, and with relation to firearms the government does this zealously. According to the federal code at the time of the publishing of this book, you can sell a personal firearm as long as it cannot be shown that you are in the business of selling firearms, and the sale is not for the sole purpose of making a profit. Selling one or two a year is safe if you are trying to reduce your collection, or maybe to get rid of a firearm you no longer want. Selling one or two a month will probably cause you to be investigated. More frequent sales without a license will probably involve an arrest.

Federal law states that people who buy and sell guns for profit be licensed, and licensed dealers must perform background checks on every sale they make. This licensing law is very strictly enforced. If you buy multiple guns monthly for resale, the Bureau of Alcohol, Tobacco, Firearms, and Explosives/BATFE will check you out, and you had better have a license. There is no federal regulation that requires a private individual to "register" their firearms, nor do most states. Some states may require you to notify law enforcement that you purchased a pistol, but that is not the norm.

Because the only people who are allowed to sell a firearm without performing a background check are individuals selling personal guns, the "gun show loop-hole" applies only when a private individual sells a gun to another private individual. If a law is created to prohibit private transactions, it also could conceivably cover passing down a family heirloom. The only practical way to stop or regulate this sort of private sale or transfer is mandatory nationwide gun registration. Otherwise how would the government know that two private individuals participated in a firearm transaction?

Remember, sales of firearms bought with the intent to sell at a profit are already required to be done only by licensed retailers with background checks performed.

Another aspect you must be aware of is that when each gun is manufactured it is registered by documenting the buyer's information and firearm serial number. This also occurs when a licensed dealer sells the firearm to an individual. If a firearm is used in a crime, the BATFE will look up the serial number to see who bought the gun from the Federal Firearms License (FFL) dealer. They can then start investigating and sometimes are able to track the firearm owner to owner all the way to the last person who owned that gun at the time the firearm was used in a crime. I personally have been asked about a firearm I sold, and I sold it to an FFL dealer. If you sell a privately owned firearm to a citizen, I would suggest you create some sort of document that has the buyer's name, contact information, and the firearm's serial number, make, and model. If you have this information, the government's tracking process is quite simple. If not, you could have to answer some hard questions regarding the firearm.

Federal Law

There are both state and federal laws concerning firearms. There is also a great amount of Internet and gun store gossip concerning these laws. Take machine guns, silencers, and "destructive devices" as examples. Federal law includes some specific (and expensive) provisions for private ownership.

Yes, I said it; you can own a machine gun (if your state law also allows it). However, there are very detailed laws concerning owning a machine gun, and just owning certain parts without the proper licenses and tax stamp can bring jail time and huge fines. It is important to note that individual states are free to ban items like those listed above if they chose to, and federal law can ban the carrying of weapons in places the state might not. You must get proper information from a credible source about firearm laws in your area and then verify the information.

Disclaimer: Even though you may be able to legally own a short barrel "sawed-off" shotgun, a fully automatic firearm gun, or a suppressor, if you choose to *carry* it for self-protection. You risk enhanced legal consequences if you are forced to use it. Besides the legal risks and public relations nightmare, these guns are extremely expensive and you most likely will not get them back if they are confiscated by government authorities.

Liability

Most people are aware that it is easy to be included in a lawsuit. Restaurants have been sued because their coffee was too hot or their food made people fat. Can you imagine how easy it would be to be sued if you shot someone? Many states have laws that allow your attacker to sue you after you lawfully defended yourself from the attacker's illegal action.

Some states have laws that may shield you from this type of lawsuit; however, all states allow you to be sued for negligent actions with your handgun if you injure or kill an innocent party. As a matter of fact, if you acted recklessly or carelessly it most likely is a criminal offense.

No matter the location and no matter the reason, you will always be held accountable for the bullets you fire. If you miss your target and break a window, it is your fault. If you shoot a bullet that goes through your attacker and kills a dog, it is your fault that the dog died. Think of your bullets like toothpaste—if you press too hard on the tube and squirt out too much toothpaste, you cannot put it back into the tube. It is the same with the bullets loaded in your handgun.

Not everyone can handle that type of responsibility, and that is perfectly fine. If you cannot do so comfortably, donate the money you were going to use to buy your handgun to the Fraternal Order of Police, because you should not own a firearm for personal protection.

Chapter 3

Safety

Four Fundamental Safety Rules

Safety around firearms is essential. It's not hard to be safe around firearms; it just takes the knowledge of basic safety rules and a little common sense. There are many variations of safety rules taught by different organizations, but they all encompass the same thoughts and goals. The following rules are commonly called the four fundamental safety rules.

1. Treat Every Weapon as if It Were Loaded

This rule is sometimes overzealously and incorrectly taught as "load every firearm." This is not what it means. This rule means that, even if you believe the firearm is unloaded, always act as if it is loaded.

Firearms are designed to be loaded, just like a car is designed to be filled with gas. Whenever you handle a firearm you should automatically check to see if it is loaded.

It is generally not possible to tell if a weapon is loaded just by looking at it. If you always treat a firearm as if it were loaded, you will always treat it with the respect it demands, which leads right to the second rule.

2. Never Point a Weapon at Anything You Do Not Intend to Shoot

Firearms are tools, and like any tool they have a purpose. A firearm's purpose is to punch holes in things. You would never use a saw on something you did not want to cut, or hit something with a sledge hammer that you did not wish to break. It is the same with a firearm. If you always treat a firearm as if it were loaded, you will always keep it pointed in a safe direction, so that if it were to negligently discharge, the round would impact on a safe(er) area.

3. Keep Your Weapon's Safety On until You Are Ready to Fire

If your firearm is equipped with an external safety device, never disengage it until you are ready to cause your firearm to discharge a bullet. There have been many instances where people have disengaged safety devices while their firearm was in the holster and then proceeded to shoot themselves while drawing the

21

firearm from the holster. Do not turn off a safety device until the firearm is actually pointed at the target.

It is also best to think of the safety as an enhancement and not the primary safety provider. Never rely on a safety to protect you from careless handling. A mechanical safety could malfunction. If you have ever had a light bulb blow out, a tire go flat, or an appliance to break you know that nothing we build is perfect and things wear out.

Figure 3.01
Keep Your Finger off
the Trigger

4. Keep Your Finger Straight and Off the Trigger until You Intend to Fire

The placing of your finger on the trigger should be the very last action you take before firing your handgun. Your finger should never be on the actual trigger unless you are engaged in the process of sending a round downrange.

As soon as you are done firing, your finger should be immediately taken off the trigger and laid along the frame of the firearm. This helps ensure that a bullet is not discharged accidentally. Humans have a flinch response that causes them to clinch their hands when startled. If your finger was on the trigger while you were walking with a firearm and you tripped, you would instinctively pull the trigger. With your finger outside the trigger guard and alongside the frame of the weapon, this will not happen.

There are other important rules common to firearm usage, or even specific shooting disciplines: e.g., no ammunition present when cleaning; keep gun unloaded at range until you are on line; clean gun after usage. You may even create other rules as you see fit. Anything that makes you safer with a firearm is acceptable. Nothing will completely reduce accidents; however, these four rules will greatly increase your safety while you are using your firearms.

Ignorance/Carelessness

Ignorance and carelessness are the two main causes of handgun accidents. Both can be avoided. Neither have a place around firearms.

Ignorance is a lack of knowledge. No one should operate a firearm without knowing the basic safety rules or how to operate that specific gun. No moral judgment is affixed to the ignorance of a person when it applies to firearms. Firearm usage must be learned. But no matter who the person is, he or she should not be allowed unsupervised access to a firearm until they have proven themselves knowledgeable in the safe use of the firearm.

Carelessness is when someone knows the safety rules but fails to follow them. Firearms do not discharge themselves. If all people followed basic safety rules, handgun accidents would not happen. Carelessness is the cause of most negligent discharges by experienced gun users. Carelessness does not have to happen. No matter how long you have used firearms or how much you know, you must always respect them as the powerful tool they are.

Unsafe Acts on Public Ranges

Something that I have noticed when dealing with firearm enthusiasts are how—as a group—they are much more safety conscious than many other groups of people. If you are on a public or private range and you inadvertently break a safety rule, someone will probably politely remind you of your breach of protocol. I have never known this to be done impolitely, even though, depending on the danger posed to others, it may be done with differing levels of firmness or urgency. This correction is done because it only takes a second for a negligent discharge to cause a life-altering injury.

Shooters, as a rule, are very polite people. They deal with people how they want to be treated. So please take any safety advice to heart. By the same token, if you see an unsafe act on a range and calmly and politely call attention to it, your warning will almost always be taken to heart. It is pretty embarrassing to a shooter to be called out, but any true firearm aficionado will respect the concern, especially if done in a professional manner.

As always, though, not every man with a firearm is a shooter, just like not every man with a piano is a concert pianist. If you are on a range and see an unsafe act, and for any reason feel like you cannot or should not correct it, then you should just leave the range until the knucklehead is finished. (It shouldn't take long, they tend to shoot a box or two of bullets just as fast as they can and rarely take the time to pick up their trash.)

Accidents Happen/How to Deal

Without attempting to scare anyone, I must state that nothing will ever eliminate handgun accidents. Recreational firearm usage is one of the safest sports, and following the fundamental rules and using common sense will reduce accidents to negligible levels. However, if you deal with firearms long enough, it is possible that you will be in the vicinity of a negligent discharge.

Do not be shocked if this happens at some point when you are on a firing range. If you are shooting at a range and a negligent discharge occurs, follow these simple steps. Take your finger off the trigger, yell cease fire, keep your firearm pointed in a safe direction, and ensure you and everyone else are okay. As with all aspects of gun use, control the situation, don't let it control you.

Storage

It is your responsibility to store your firearms where they are not accessible to unauthorized persons. No one not properly trained should ever be allowed unsupervised access to a gun. This does not necessarily mean that everyone with access to a gun needs a formal course or supervision from a certified instructor. But it does mean that *you* are responsible for *your* guns, and you must not allow anyone access to your firearms without ensuring they understand gun safety.

You can go out to the range with your spouse or your children and show them the safe way to operate your firearm. It is your job to ensure that people using your gun are supervised and are safe.

Handguns should be stored unloaded and separate from ammunition. In our home we have a gun safe in one room, and in another we store a lockable wooden ammo crate that holds our ammunition. The keys are in separate locations to keep interested parties from opening both at the same time. For the sake of your guns, handguns should be stored in a cool, dry place. This prevents rust or corrosion.

You must be aware that if you own firearms, you are responsible for your firearms, even if they are stored. This is both a legal and a moral responsibility. You may be charged criminally if minors gain access to your firearms.

With this in mind, your individual personal situation will dictate the level of security you invest in your firearm storage. A person living alone does not have the same set of concerns as a person living in a house full of people. When I was fresh out of the

Marines and living alone on a large farm, I kept guns all over the house. I may or may not have even had a few duct-taped under tables and in plastic bags in the toilet tank. Of course now that I have young children that visit my home, I cannot live this way, amd I must secure my handguns.

Storage Devices

There are many different firearm storage devices such as:

- Cabinets
- Safes
- Hard cases
- Gun rugs
- Strong boxes
- Trigger guards
- Cable locks
- Internal locks within the firearms themselves

Some Common Storage Devices

These devices are used to deny access to unauthorized individuals. They do not always prevent theft; sometimes they only make theft more difficult. You must also remember that mechanical devices such as trigger locks or cables are subject to failure. They are also not meant to keep a self-defense firearm ready for use and should never be placed on a loaded weapon!

Figure 3.02
Some Common Storage Devices

Home Defense Guns

A general rule is that any firearm not in use should be securely stored. However, common sense dictates that we never know when and where we may be in a self-defense shooting.

If I had prior knowledge that someone was going to attempt to kill me I would make darn sure I showed up late to the appointment. If you feel the need of a self-defense firearm, it can always be thought of as "in-use," because you can never know when an attack might occur. For my personal situation, I have a revolver as well as a 12-gauge shotgun that are considered home-defense firearms. Everything else is unloaded and stored away from its ammunition.

If you choose to keep a loaded home defense firearm, you must ask yourself, "Does the convenience of a loaded gun outweigh the danger of having it around?" If a gun is kept loaded in the home, it is the responsibility of the owner to make it inaccessible to unauthorized individuals. Remember, safety *first*, and every gun should be treated as if it is loaded. Again, never place a trigger lock or other device on a loaded self-defense gun, this makes it unsafe and may cause the firearm to discharge when you try to take it off.

Kids and Guns

As a firearm instructor, I often hear from people that they would like to own a gun, but their spouse will not allow it because they have children in the house. On a grand scale, I understand this *feeling*. However, when emotion is taken out of the discussion and the facts are examined, it's less reasonable.

Children can be injured by common house current, but does your spouse say that you must live without electricity? Or, do they insist only on having child locks on the electric outlets? More children are injured in motor vehicle accidents than in firearm-related accidents but probably own at least one car.

It's a parent's job to keep his or her children safe, and no one wants to bring something into the home that is dangerous to his or her child. I agree with anyone that believes that one of a parent's primary responsibilities is to ensure their child's safety. I do not think that the mere presence of a firearm in the home makes that home inherently more dangerous than a non-firearm household. With proper education, storage, and supervision, firearms are no more dangerous than any other tool.

I am not in the habit of making broad statements on how others should act. Generally, I teach options and explain the reasons for using each of those options. I prefer to let you decide based on the application of facts to your personal situation. I can tell you how I deal with the issue of guns in my home with my child and, hopefully, give perspective to other parents who question guns in the home.

When I was growing up, my parents were not anti-gun, but they were anti-me-having-a-gun. There were guns in my home. My dad was a law enforcement officer and, as such, always had at least one handgun in the home. My father subscribed to the "old school" policy on kids and guns. Dad said, "Boy, I've got a gun in that closet, and I better never catch you playing with it, or I'll make you wish you hadn't." Well, being the bright child that I was, I figured that meant he just didn't want to *catch* me. As long as I put it back *exactly* as I found it, I could pose in the mirror in my best gunfighter stance whenever I was alone in the house. Luckily, I never fired the pistol into the mirror or myself. I guess the massive gun handling skills I learned from TV and movies kept me from accidentally firing the gun, but I'd bet it was just *dumb* luck. As I got older, dad did take me out shooting once or twice. We even went hunting once, but I was never allowed to have my own gun so I always had that curiosity. I think mom still thinks I wouldn't be so interested in guns if I got to shoot them more as a kid.

I imagine that, even if there were no guns in my home and if my parents forbid me to even mention guns, I would have found someone to let me see one. (It happened just like that with a motorcycle, but since Mom still doesn't know about that, we won't get into details ...)

In my house, we have a smart and independent 7-year-old girl. She thinks for herself and is not afraid to abandon what she has been told if she thinks she knows better.

The first step I have taken to keep her safe is to do my best to stop her from being able to access the firearms if she chooses to disregard my gun rules. This is not foolproof. Kids have an uncanny ability to find what they are looking for. I am sure that at some point in her life, she will find the gun safe keys.

For the second step, we have taught her the NRA's Eddie Eagle gun safety rules. This strategy is to teach the child what to do if they find a gun. The rules are simple and effective.

Eddie Eagle says if the child sees a gun, they should:

- Stop
- Don't touch
- Leave the area
- Tell an adult

These rules are particularly important, as over 50% of American households have firearms in them. If she is visiting a friend's house, we do not want her to try to tell another child not to play with a gun, as that might cause that child to point the gun at our child to tease her. We want her safely away from any unsecured gun, not to act like she is in charge of it.

The last thing we do is to take away her curiosity. My wife and I took her to the range, and she watched her momma shoot a pistol. I sat with our child and explained to her about guns and answered all her questions. This did not work too well because, even with hearing protection, my child thought the handguns were too loud. She did not want to be around them. We then got her a BB rifle. We let her shoot it under supervision when she asks to, but she doesn't really like it very much. Furthermore, we don't force her, but she knows that if she wants to shoot, she can shoot as long as she asks and her mother or I take her to an appropriate location.

This works well for us. We keep the guns in a locked safe and the ammo locked in a separate room. (This does not include our personal carry firearms; they are kept out of reach and locked up separately from the stored firearms.)

After we taught our child the basic firearm safety rules, we then taught her what to do if she encountered a firearm outside our home. The last step in taking away her curiosity was to expose her to firearms and what they can do and allow her the privilege to own her very own BB rifle that she can use when supervised. As she gets older, we plan on increasing her exposure to firearms, but at this point we think she is only ready for the basics.

She likes to say she shoots and likes to mortify her grandma with stories of how she goes shooting with her very own pistol. But in reality she has gone exactly one time, and she owns no firearm. She also gets plenty of opportunity to go to the range, but each time she's asked if she wants to shoot, she is too busy coloring and says she will shoot next time. This is great because there is no taboo for her to explore.

As the parent, you are the best judge of what your child is ready for. This is only a guideline for when your child asks about guns for the first time. For us, it was when my wife told me to look out the window, and our little girl was on the porch with a rubber training pistol in one hand, a rubber training knife in the other, and yelling at the family dog (which she named Shotgun), "Pay attention! I am trying to give you a class!" My wife told me I had created a monster. It served to reinforce in my mind the responsibility I have to be a positive role model for my child. If I am unsafe in my attitude toward guns, I can be sure my child will take notice.

Chapter 4

What Happens in a Gunfight

"A lifetime of training for just ten seconds."
— Jesse Owens

Gunfights are dynamic. They are ever changing. Gunfights are loud, uncomfortable, and dangerous. Set aside any notions of glory or excitement. Even if you survive a gunfight (and that is the sole objective), you still must face defending your actions to the police and attorneys in the legal system. It is also likely you must defend your actions to your family, friends, and coworkers on an ethical level. We are going to go over some common changes that may happen to you during the stress of a lethal force situation.

Statistics Are Not Gospel

Before we get into the changes, both physical and mental, that may occur during a gunfight, I would like to state that these changes may not happen to every person every time. No gunfight is the same. It is common to hear in a firearm class that the statistically average gunfight is less than 2.5 seconds long, 2.5 rounds are fired, and the distance is less than 7 yards. This does not mean that every gunfight follows these statistics. As an example, let's imagine 10 gunfights. Of these 10 imaginary gunfights, 9 where at 1 yard and one was at 61 yards. The average would be 7 yards. Notice, there wasn't a single 7-yard gunfight in the above example. Statistically, 85% of gunfights are within 10 feet. Most of those are at near contact distances.

Statistics are averages, not gospel. Statistically, you're not ever going to be in a lethal force situation, but statistics won't help when you are being shot at. What statistics do give is a picture of likely happenings. The following are to be taken that way. These responses may or may not occur in your situation, but knowing about them will make you better able to cope if they do happen.

Stress Response

In medical terms, stress is a physical or psychological stimulus that can produce mental or physiological reactions. Stress can be both good and bad. For our purposes, the "fight or flight" reaction caused by encountering stress is both. Your body's dumping of adrenaline and norepinephrine into the bloodstream prepares the body for either battle or retreat. This response has been accepted since 1929 when it was first described by Walter Cannon.

Physical and Mental Changes

While the body's preparations allow for a temporary increase of physical strength, increased ability to produce energy and process oxygen, and in some cases increased acuteness of the senses, these reactions do have drawbacks. The same physical reactions cause negative symptoms, also. These symptoms are caused by a reaction by the autonomic nervous system and are involuntary. We are going to address some of the most relevant symptoms. As I said before you may not experience all or any of these, nor will a person necessarily experience the same ones each time they are exposed to extreme stress. But you need to understand the stress responses, not only so you can deal with them, but so you can recover from them and know that what happened to you is normal.

Trembling or Shaking of Muscles

Your body's adrenaline dump will prepare your muscles for hard use; however, the increased blood flow, increased energy, and mental stimulation will also cause muscle trembling. If you have ever been really frightened you probably had "the shakes" afterward.

Loss of Dexterity

A common training statement is, "In a fight, fingers turn to flippers." This means that your hands will fumble and you have to use gross motor skills and big movements instead of fine motor skills.

Digestive/Urinary Symptoms

Relaxation of bladder and bowels, and diarrhea are normal. This is not mentioned often and is denied even more often. If this happens to you after someone tries to kill you, you are normal. Do not be ashamed. Just imagine how the first person felt that "had the poop scared out of them." At least you'll know that it's normal, and if that's the worse thing that happened after somebody tried to kill you, then you won.

Impaired Thinking

The code red, adrenalin-reinforced mind is not the same kitchen table, drive-the-kids-to-school mindset that you have during white or yellow levels of awareness. For our entire lives we have been taught that murder is wrong, and we as a society have internalized this to the point that we may not be able to grasp the reality that "Hey, this guy is trying to *kill* me!"

This can cause something called cognitive dissonance, where the mind tries to reconcile two equally believed thoughts—in this case, the belief that people do not kill and the fact that a person is trying to kill you. This is the reason that people who survive lethal force encounters say things like, "I don't know what happened; it all just happened so fast I just couldn't think." A denial response may also occur, such as, "This cannot be happening to me …" It is possible in extreme situations for someone to go into a catatonic or zombie-like state; your mind can completely shut down. This is something that training can deal with, and the more mental programming you do by training, the less likely this is to happen.

Sometimes in cognitive dissonance things of minor importance can take on a great importance. This is how your mind attempts to cope. Have you ever been in a very bad car wreck and your spouse worries about the ambulance crew seeing her with her hair a mess? This is not vanity; it is a coping mechanism. You must be aware of this, however. Because of cognitive dissonance you may recall some trivial matter, like scratching the slide of your pistol, with greater detail and seeming concern than you recall the dead body of your attacker and why you were forced to shoot him or her to save your life. This may be taken out of context and methods for dealing with this will be discussed later.

It is also possible to have what seems like an out-of-body experience. You may have a sense of disconnection; it is even possible to fire shots and not remember ever firing your weapon. This topic is discussed in depth in a book I highly recommend, *Deadly Force Encounters* by Dr. Artwohl and Loren W. Christensen.

Temporary Blindness

Hysterical blindness is rare and generally happens to the untrained. Basically, the individual experiencing hysterical blindness is so scared that his or her brain simply refuses to see the stressor anymore. Normally this reaction also occurs in tandem with a panicked fleeing of the scene.

Tunnel Vision

Tunnel vision is the narrowing of the field of view to the most obvious threat. This can cause obvious problems such as not seeing other threats, or not noticing innocent bystanders in the line of fire. This symptom can blind you to other options such as cover.

Unlike some other symptoms, this one has options. Have you ever watched well-trained combat shooters on the range? After they fire they bring the handguns to their chests (muzzle pointed downrange) and, using exaggerated movements, turn their heads to the right and to the left.

This movement is done to break tunnel vision and to scan for additional threats. It is a skill that you must practice, even though it seems simple. Too many simply go through the motions and do not actually *see* to the sides when they are performing this action. Make a point to look and recognize what is behind you when you do this. Have a partner hold up fingers and call out how many he or she is exposing.

Auditory Exclusion

Auditory exclusion is similar to tunnel vision. It affects hearing in the same way as tunnel vision affects sight. Individuals involved in live shooting have reported barely hearing the shots. These same people firing the same gun on a firing range experience pain from the report of the firearm if they do not wear hearing protection. If you hunt or know hunters it is common for them not to wear hearing protection in the field. This is the same as the police or the military. These same people faithfully wear hearing protection on the ranges shooting the very same weapons they carry in "real life."

It is common for them not to be bothered by a gunshot when placed in a stressful situation. This might be positive, except the same effect will also keep you from hearing warnings yelled to you. "Hey! Watch Out," "He's behind you," "Stop! Police!" are all things it would behoove you to hear. A good way to break auditory exclusion is to forcibly give verbal commands to your threat to retreat or drop the weapon. This communication on your part not only reduces your physical stress-related symptoms, but also firmly reinforces your desire to not be the aggressor.

Tachypsychia (Temporal Distortion)

This is the effect of seeing an incident occurring in slow motion. When both the visual portion of your brain and your gross motor control are accelerated, your actions can seem to speed up, and your stressor's actions can seem to slow down. Have you ever been in a car accident and everything seems to be happening in slow motion? Tachypsychia is why stressful situations are sometimes perceived this way. A person's temporal distortion is believed to function more effectively the higher the individual's level of training.

The study of the effect of stressors on a person's body is relatively new as a scientific field; and the study effect of stressors on a person's mind is even newer. Basically, the more training and *repetition* a person has done in advance, the less these things affect them in a life or death situation. But as entire books have been written on each little paragraph above, you may want to spend some time researching this in depth. Massad Ayoob, Loren Christenson, Lt. Col. Dave Grossman, and Dr. Alexis Artwohl are all excellent authors on this subject, but are by no means the only resources in this field.

Chapter 5

Use of Force

Responsibility

For each right you claim, you inherit an equally important responsibility. When a boy gets his first rifle, not only does he get the great privilege of using a rifle, but he also becomes responsible for how he uses the rifle. The most clichéd version of this balance of rights and responsibilities is the adage, "You can't yell fire in a crowded theater."

It is true that, as an American, you have the right to say most anything you desire, but you also have the responsibility to speak the truth and not to promote panic. The right to keep and bear arms is often mentioned, but the responsibility for each bullet fired is not often mentioned.

Neither the intended consequence nor the reasons or justifications behind the firing matter. What matters is the result. As an adult you must accept the responsibility for your actions. You accepted the privileges, so is it not also fair for you to accept the consequences as well?

A saying my child hears when she refuses to acknowledge that her actions have reactions is, "You can do anything you're big enough to handle, but you have to be big enough to take the praise or the licks." All too often we as a society fail to see this as a part of life. There is a clamoring in the halls of our government buildings to legislate everything from marijuana to marriage. Everyone wants to be protected from the results of problems without having to bear the ugly task of *dealing* with the problems.

Today it is commonplace to hear people wanting what is owed them. "It's not fair!" "It's my right!" "I only want what they got!" All these statements ignore the realm of personal responsibility. That might be a strong opinion, but is that not reasonable when we demand a greater freedom of action?

We advocate self-protection. We teach people how to do what they believe is necessary to protect their families. As such, we are held to a higher standard. We choose not to be victimized; therefore, we must take great care not to victimize others. This thought of personal responsibility is central to the philosophy of the Shepherd School.

Reasonableness

Reasonableness means you are just in your actions, that other people with reason (the ability to know right from wrong) would take similar actions in similar circumstances. Any research you may do on the use of force will always be based on the fact that, to be legal, an action must be reasonable.

The problem with the reasonableness standard is that it can be vague. There is no "fine line" or mechanical definition of what is or is not reasonable. The Supreme Court has also held in *Graham v. Connor*, 490 U.S. 386 (1989) that, as far as police officers are concerned, "The reasonableness of a particular use of force must be judged from the perspective of a reasonable officer on the scene, and its calculus must embody an allowance for the fact that police officers are often forced to make split-second decisions about the amount of force necessary in a particular situation." This has some bearing on the civilian, as it shows the legal theory behind what is considered reasonable and what is not.

Always remember that your use of force is going to be judged by persons not on the scene. You are not going to be the one to decide if your actions were justified. A judge or at the very least the prosecutor for your jurisdiction will look over your actions and decide if they were reasonable. The following sections outline some ideas to illustrate what would make you appear reasonable.

Attitude

At one time I liked to think of myself as a "tough guy." I wanted others to think of me as a "tough guy" also. You might say I was a poser, but I really enjoyed telling the ladies (before I married my wife) that I was a 6'3", 250-pound, former Marine, that now worked as a maximum security prison guard. I also liked carrying in my pocket a spent bullet dug out of a clay bank. When I was in the "tough-guy" mood and wanted to impress myself, I would take it out and casually toss it at whoever was bothering me. When they caught it I loved to say, "Keep it up and the next one's coming a lot faster."

To make matters worse, I didn't even own a pistol at that time. Now that a lot of time has passed and my ego is not as fragile, and I have gained an extra bit of maturity, I realize how stupid and dangerous a remark like that actually is.

Big egos and negative attitudes have no place in the minds of those who carry firearms. If you ever get involved in a shooting, a stupid remark or a careless action could cause you to be sent to prison. Worse than that, they can cause a lifetime of regret and pain, both for you and for the family of the person you shot.

What You Say, How You Look

Right or wrong, what you say and how you look play a part in the minds of the people you deal with. Studies have been done in stores to see the level of service customers receive based on their personal appearances. If you take the extra time to strap on your pistol, take an extra second to make sure that you look the part of an upstanding model citizen and not Homeless Joe.

If you would like a better example, look at one of the many websites for celebrity mug shots. The actors always look guilty in their mug shots; they normally do not get any sympathy. They also look the worst we have ever seen them. I am not saying that it is right to think this way, just that it is a reality.

Any Fight Is a Gun Fight

Something that you might hear if you take a use-of-force class or a handgun carry course is, "If you carry a gun, every fight is a gunfight, because you brought a gun." What happens if you get in a fistfight with no intention of using deadly force, but you get knocked down and your firearm is taken from you? What would happen if you are fighting and the weapon just "prints" its outline against your clothes and the police are called?

Politeness

If you exercise your right to carry a gun, you will be held to a higher standard. This is as it should be, as you will have on your person the means to employ deadly force. Simply stated, you have the ability to kill. If you carry a gun, you had better be more polite, more courteous, and more careful than you are when you are disarmed, because one mistake can not only cost someone their life, but it could cost you your freedom.

Shoot to Wound/Kill/Neutralize

I talk a lot about lethal force, and one concept comes up almost universally. I call this idea the leg-shot syndrome. The leg-shot syndrome is illustrated by the statement, "I wouldn't aim to kill; I would shoot the robber in the leg." I believe I know where this thought comes from. It comes from the fact that all firearm instructors I know try very hard to give firearms classes only to the "good guys." As a rule, "good guys" don't go around killing, robbing, and raping people. They believe that everyone has redeeming qualities. Good guys don't want to kill people, they don't start deadly force encounters, and if they had their way, the bad guys would not be bad.

Now before I get tons of hate mail, let me say that I understand the reason people think this, and I wish everyone in the world felt this way. If there were no bad guys, there would be no crime. I could then put more energy into my primary job of preparing for natural disasters instead of diverting energy to preparing for criminal disasters. While understanding and admiring this idea, I want to emphasize that this is not a good way to apply this concept.

There are many reasons why the philosophy of shooting to wound is not sound in the lethal force arena. Some of the reasons are legal, some tactical, and some, yes, are moral. I will begin with what I hear as the most widely used reason: the legal aspect of deadly force.

A handgun is a lethal weapon. Unlike a baseball bat, a butcher knife, or a policeman's baton, there is no absolutely 100% non-lethal way to use a handgun against another human. When a metal projectile strikes human flesh at supersonic speeds, things happen. It is entirely possible to shoot someone in an area of the body that contains no vital organs, but have the bullet ricochet into a vital organ or an artery. Because of this the law does not distinguish the difference between shooting a person in the head and shooting a person in the foot. If there is not a legally defensible justification for lethal force, and you shoot someone, you are now a criminal. A bullet cannot be recalled once it leaves the barrel, and the damage it does upon entering a person cannot be decided by the person who fired the bullet.

A physical reason not to shoot to wound is that tactically manipulating a firearm under lethal force pressure is extremely hard. Quite a few books and statistics from a vast amount of historical data show that less than 1/3 of the rounds fired in a gunfight impact on the target (meaning 2/3 miss the person entirely). This is bad, but wait until you realize that other statistics that show approximately 90% of gun fights happen under 3 meters.

If the vast majority of people involved in a gunfight (including professionals) completely miss a person at almost contact distance, how realistic is it to think that you are going to hit one of your attacker's smallest targets, especially since those tiny targets are most likely moving? Is this reasonable?

Tennessee (and every other state I have found that has a defined handgun training curriculum) specifies shooting center-mass with the intent to stop. This involves two concepts. The first concept is to always aim for center-mass. This means aiming your projectile to impact inside the largest target area exposed (normally the chest). Because this is the largest area, you have the greatest ability to actually hit the target. Also, a shot to the chest area has the highest probability of stopping your attacker because it is the location of most the body's organs.

Intent to stop is the other concept. It is neither aiming to kill nor shooting to wound. Either of these is irrelevant. Your ability to apply lethal force self-defense is centered on the attacker being able to kill you or being in the process of trying to kill you.

If the mere presence of your legally owned firearm causes the attacker to stop, it has done its job. If one well-placed round to center mass persuades the criminal to stop, that's okay; however, if it takes 5 boxes of bullets to stop a drug crazed, gang-banging, Neo-Nazi terrorist from killing you, hey, so be it. Once deadly force is employed, the goal is stopping the attack, and the amount of force is irrelevant as long it is needed. However, you must also know that once the attacker either loses the ability or the will to kill you, your justification to legally employ lethal force ends. Your goal is to neutralize, not to kill.

I don't shoot to kill, I shoot to live. If my attacker stops trying to kill me, I get to live. I like that.

An old law enforcement joke goes like this. A cop on the stand was asked by the lawyer why he shot his client 16 times. The old timer drawled, well, cause 15 wasn't enough and 17 would have been too much....

This intent to stop is only half of my moral argument. The other reason comes from plain street sense. I have a few years of

experience working in the corrections system. These years have
been split between entry-level corrections working on the
recreation yards and cages listening to inmates talk about
themselves and their crimes, and working as a supervisor in
maximum security units and applying inmate psychological
knowledge to keep the prison running smoothly. Criminals do
what they do because it works for them.

If a mugger or a rapist tries to talk you into leaving with him,
it's because it has always worked for him before. Believe me; a
violent criminal hasn't decided to start being a violent criminal
just because you're there. A criminal starts small and works up,
gradually becoming more violent. If a criminal gets away with
hurting you, he will do it to someone else. I am not saying that
vigilante justice is okay; because it's not. I am not advocating
deadly force as a punishment for a criminal, either.

What I am saying is that you are a reasonable person, with an
inalienable right to life and liberty, minding your own business,
living a peaceful life. You have a right to do what you need to do
to be safe, to go home to your family. If you are a victim of an
unprovoked attack, where a criminal is trying to kill you for his
personal gain, then you are not wrong for wanting to stop him
from hurting you. You should never feel bad about wanting to get
back to your family safely. Your family needs you; make sure you
do what needs to be done to be there for them.

Some States' Laws Require New Threat Assessments for Every Round Fired.

Whether the law states this explicitly or not, there is an
understanding that you are responsible for each round of
ammunition fired. If you blindly squeeze off rounds without
considering where they will go, you will likely spend some time
behind bars. At the very least, firing a weapon without a valid
reason (that you can verbalize and is deemed reasonable) for each
shot will have someone else living in your house with you still
paying the mortgage.

After a Shooting

For the sake of argument, let's assume that you bought a
handgun, got some training, and became licensed to carry. Let's
further assume you were attacked, and, being a well-trained
person with the proper mindset and adequate equipment, you

prevailed and ended the encounter with no more holes than when you started. Your attacker did not fair so well. The display of your weapon and your verbal challenge went unheeded, and the criminal continued his attack and ultimately forced you to shoot him to protect your own life. He's down and bleeding; now what do you do?

Most people assume that, in the event of a self-defense shooting, their responsibility ends with the shooting. An armed citizen buys a handgun, trains in its use, earns a carry permit, gets attacked, defends himself, and survives. It is pretty reasonable to assume that the cycle is over. Unfortunately, it's not. A new cycle begins in which people begin to pick apart the citizen's actions and decide, using the benefits of hindsight and comfort, what a person did instantly and under the stress of a lethal encounter. The police, the prosecutor, judge, and possibly a jury will decide the citizen's fate. As tools to judge his or her fate, they will use the actions of the armed citizen before, during and after the incident.

Many people, myself included, earn a living studying and teaching the art and science of the actions to take before and during a self-defense encounter. Individuals are not even legally allowed to become armed citizens unless they prove that they will live up to the standards imposed on them. They must be sane, responsible, free of felony convictions, and cannot have committed certain misdemeanors.

Proper tactics to use in a gunfight are also well documented. Anybody with five dollars can buy a book or magazine discussing tactics and strategies that will help him or her survive a gunfight. Not so well known are the actions to take after a self-defense shooting incident.

A citizen can feel that he or she was threatened, and that he or she had no option but to fight back using lethal force. But if the police, the district attorney, and the media decide that the citizen's feeling of threat was not justified, the upstanding citizen becomes a suspect and faces the possibility of becoming a convicted felon.

In the next few pages we will describe some actions a person should take if they are ever involved in a shooting. The acronym CAPS will help you remember the steps. I like this principle so well that I have incorporated it into all of my civilian shooting courses. I will not only describe the acronym here, but I will add some of my own thoughts and how I arrived at them.

Call the Police

If you have to *draw*, make the *call!*

You did not do anything wrong. You were attacked. Likely the only reason you were not injured was that you had a gun. People who were attacked call the police. Guilty people hide their actions from the police. The prisons are full of people who did not see witnesses and left the scene, only to be described later at trial as a guilty person who ruthlessly shot an innocent civilian and then fled the scene.

Flight equals guilt in our legal system. If this is not reason enough to call the police, let's look at another common theme of our system of justice. It is that the first man to make a complaint is right; the other is wrong. If you were involved in a shooting and then called the police, and while you are on line with the dispatcher, a friend of the attacker called the police claiming you attacked him. The police will obviously investigate, but because you have already made a report it's a lot easier to believe you're the victim. Imagine that you did not call, that you followed bad gun shop advice, looked around, picked up your fired casings, and left the scene. What would happen if someone reported you as the shooter, and the police found you carrying a pistol that matched the bullets in a dead man? Your bad day just got worst.

Even if you were not forced to shoot your attacker, still call the police; the criminal or even a bystander may have called the police. The only way you know the police have the true and accurate account of your innocence is if you are the one to tell them!

There are a lot of theories concerning how much you should tell the police in the event of a shooting. This is important, and we will discuss that in a few minutes, but for right now you need to realize that your lawful, reasonable, and legally justified use of force is in an entirely different realm than some street crud being interviewed by the police for his third liquor store robbery. You're not a criminal so *don't act like one!*

Assist the Injured (Yourself and Others)

Justified self-defense means someone tried to kill you. Bullets, broken bottles, baseball bats, or Bowie knives were just used against you. After the smoke clears, you're going to see if you're okay. Also, because you're a decent human being, you're going to make sure none of the innocent bystanders are hurt.

I want you to consider assisting your attacker with first aid. You are going to do this because you are a decent human being who does not want to hurt anyone. You don't want to kill people. You were attacked, and you defended yourself. Now that the fight is over, you are back to being full of peace and love. Now you should not run over to a drugged up street thug holding a knife in his hand and cursing you at the top of his lungs. You should not do anything to risk your own safety. However, if you can safely do so, you should try to help everyone who is injured.

Do not do this if there is still a threat, but if you can safely render aid, imagine what would happen in a courtroom if you could say to the jury, "I never wanted to hurt anyone. That man over there tried to kill me and I still tried to save his life. Why am I being made to look like the bad guy?" I think this is a reasonable question.

Place Your Weapon in a Safe Location

Now imagine the following scene. You've been attacked. A shooting has taken place. The police have been called. You are covered in the blood of your attacker because you have just finished bandaging his wounds. You are standing up waiting on the police with your gun in your hand so you can fully cooperate with the police when they get on scene because you know they are going to want to take the gun as evidence.

Do you want to know how the police would see the exact event? A police officer and his partner are just back from a domestic dispute. They haven't had lunch, and they both know that they have a long couple of hours left of report writing when they get a call from dispatch of a shooting a few blocks away. Not much information has been received from dispatch. They hit the lights and sirens. Their bodies get hit with a burst of adrenaline, and their minds start racing with the possible situations. They arrive on the scene to see a wild-eyed man with bloody hands and a big black handgun. They see a man on the ground, and once again their eyes focus on the man standing there with that big black handgun. Police are trained to react to the sight of a gun, and they will.

After a shooting, put your weapon back in the holster, put it on the seat of your car, or stick it in your pocket. Do something to secure it. Make no sudden moves when the police arrive, and above all, do what they say. The time (if any) to make accusations of police mistreatment is after you are cleared of all charges.

Secure the Scene

Have you seen the movie *Con-Air?* Nicolas Cage's character was found guilty of killing a man with his bare hands. In the fight scene, three men attacked him, because they disliked soldiers, liked his wife, and were generally unpleasant people. One of them also pulled out a switch-blade knife. Nicolas Cage, being the hero of the movie and being an Army Ranger fresh from Desert Storm, killed him. One of the attackers took the dead man's knife and ran off. Does anyone think that an unarmed war hero, attacked by three knife-wielding street rats, would be convicted of manslaughter? However, in the movie, because there was no weapon found, and because of his training, the judge convicted him of manslaughter.

Gang members have been known to take evidence from a scene. They have a lot more experience in dealing with crime than you do. So, if it is safe and if you can do so without substantially altering the crime scene, make sure that your attacker's weapon is present. The police will need it to clear you of wrongdoing.

What Else Should You Do?

In addition to the CAPS acronym, here are some additional thoughts of mine that might be of help to you in the event you do have to use lethal force to protect your life. First, no matter what your friend's cousin that once dated a cop told you, never under any circumstances try to fool the police by adding, taking away, or moving evidence.

If you ever shoot someone outside your house and drag the body inside, the only thing that will happen is that my friends who still work for the Department of Correction will be feeding you lunch every day for the next 20 years. The same applies to shooting a burglar and putting a kitchen knife in the burglar's hand. Have you ever seen the TV show *CSI*? It might not be the most accurate description of a crime lab, but it is based on the fact that there are such things as forensic scientists.

Policemen are not dumb. They can deduce that the knife in the dead man's hand is the same kind of knife in your kitchen butcher block, and that block is missing the exact type of knife that is in the burglar's hand. Match that with the fact that the kitchen is behind where the evidence says you were when you shot the guy, and the police will soon figure out that the dead guy in your living room could not have gotten the knife that is now in his hand. If that happens, you're in a world of hurt.

In the small town that my ex-wife is from, a family acquaintance of hers earned himself a 26-year prison sentence for a self-defense shooting. He came home to find his wife's lover waiting for him. The intruder attacked him in his own home while brandishing a knife. The citizen shot and killed his attacker, then panicked when he could not find the knife. He then placed a knife in the dead man's hand and called the police. His legal problems began when the deceased was lifted onto the gurney and the attacker's knife was found under the corpse.

There have been many cases of instances such as this, where a justified shooting was prosecuted as murder or manslaughter due to the citizen's actions after the incident. Once again, never, under any circumstance, for any reason alter the crime scene for the purpose of enhancing your story. You will get caught, and you will look like a criminal, and anything a criminal says is suspect.

Never lie to the police. Everything you say will be written down and verified. If you lie, they will find out, and you will appear guilty. If you look guilty, charges will be filed against on you. If charges are placed against you, and you look guilty, it is not a stretch of the imagination to say that you will be found guilty. The problem is that it is possible to appear to be lying when you are actually telling the truth. This is a catch 22 that should scare anyone who is considering going armed. It should not stop you, but only make you very aware of the risks that could be present.

Many physiological changes occur in your body in response to dealing with someone who is trying to kill you. We discussed these earlier in Chapter 4. Since we already know that cognitive dissonance may cause important things to seem trivial, while trivial things can seem extremely important, you may realize that this could also mean that you say things at the scene that you later realize are inaccurate. The reason for the Fifth Amendment is so that you do not incriminate yourself by saying such things.

Anybody who has ever watched a cop show knows that "pleading the fifth" is sometimes thought to be the same as saying, "I'm guilty as sin." So how does a person juggle the following factors? You cannot lie to the police. You want to cooperate. You called the police. You're the victim. You were attacked. Everything you say is going to be used against you. You just shot someone. You know going in that everything you say at the scene has a strong possibility of being wrong?

One such solution is saying something like, "Officer, I want to cooperate. I'm the one that called you, but before I talk to you, I'd like to see a doctor; I'm not feeling very well." Remember CAPS, assist the injured. You have just been in a lethal force encounter. Remember all those physiological changes mentioned previously. It's perfectly normal to want a doctor to look you over. The time it takes to get checked out by a doctor is probably all the time it will take to get a lawyer to protect your rights.

If you have any experience with doctors, you will know that they are members of one of the few legitimate professions that are not impressed with badges. When you go into the emergency room, the doctor will tell the policeman to get out of his exam room and ask you who your emergency contact is. My emergency contact knows that she is to get me a lawyer on the way to the emergency room. This is probably something worth discussing with your spouse or very trusted friend if you do decide to carry a handgun for personal protection.

To me, this is perfectly reasonable, I can articulate my reasoning and my desire to cooperate after my life-safety issue is resolved. Most cops are also going to understand (they may not like it), but if I get an officer that continues to press for a statement after I tell him I fully intend to cooperate after I see a doctor, I will just tell him that I made a simple request and if he cannot understand that my concern at this moment is my personal health after a life-threatening experience I'll demand to get a lawyer because I won't be treated like a criminal when I'm the victim.

In law enforcement training circles, it's widely known that after a lethal force event participants can lose blocks of memory concerning the event or because of those stress-related changes, have faulty memories. Evidence suggests that it takes at least two full REM sleep cycles to start getting accurate memory of the event back. If, in your rush to cooperate with the police you give a full statement on the scene based upon what you think you remember, but a week later recall the facts differently, it's going to be hard to "recant" your earlier confession. There is nothing wrong with asking for a lawyer and maintaining your innocence, just be careful of how you do it, because most of the information on how to defend your rights in police encounters is geared toward the guilty—and you're not guilty.

My last bit of information is something I learned from another firearm instructor, Clint Smith of Thunder Ranch. It was one of those "why didn't I think of that ..." ideas. He teaches that once the police arrive (because you called them), and you thank them for coming (because you are scared and you called them for help), the next words out of your mouth should be "That man attacked me officer and I want him arrested!"

Makes sense to me. If someone tries to hurt me, or otherwise tries to make me a victim of a crime, as an innocent man the first thing I will do when a cop arrives is demand his help. It does not matter if your attacker is laying on the floor with multiple 12 gauge slugs to his head. As Mr. Smith points out, you're probably not a doctor, and neither is the cop, neither you nor the cop is qualified to pronounce death. So demanding the arrest of someone who just attempted to murder you is a reasonable act. When directly asked on the stand, the officer is duty bound to report what you said to him. How do you think the jury will react if you follow the steps outlined?

You are a reasonably well-trained normal, sane, sober, law-abiding citizen who was attacked by a violent criminal. You defended yourself against an unprovoked attack, called the police, and an ambulance. You attempted to render first aid on the person who just tried to kill you because you're an honestly good person. When the police arrive you thank them for coming and demand your attacker's arrest, and then tell the good officers that you want to visit the emergency room before you give your statement because you feel ill after being attacked.

Big difference between that and the actions of some gang-banger that shoots someone, runs, and later pleads the fifth and demands a lawyer after being caught.

In conclusion, I would like to reiterate that in the event you are in a lethal force situation, your training is what will get you through. But it is your actions and lifestyle before and after the shooting that will keep you out of legal trouble. Your mental preparation and attitude are just as important as your physical skill, and these three are a hundred times more important to you than the tool strapped to your belt.

Don't Blab in the Bar

It is crucial to remember that not everyone shares the same feelings toward self-defense. You also must be aware that someone is listening all of the time. It has now become necessary to teach teenagers that what they write in an online blog today can be accessed and read years down the line by prospective employers. It is important to know that yesterday's actions can be judged in the light of tomorrow's events.

If, prior to a shooting, you brag to your coworkers about your new carry permit and how you will "waste any @#$% that messes with you," you can be sure that in the event some @#$% does attack you and you do shoot them, somebody will tell the District Attorney what you make a habit of saying. Your previous comments might be enough to turn a questionable self-defense shooting into an indictment for murder.

Your words are a window to your thoughts and what you say "can and will be used against you in a court of law." Sound familiar? Nothing you say will change an officer's mind after he put the cuffs on you, and saying stupid things that you don't mean can, in some cases, help get those cuffs locked on your wrists.

Lastly, remember that if you ever do actually get in a self-defense shooting, never discuss the situation with anyone other than your lawyer and/or your clergy. *Never* brag, never boast. Killing, even in self-defense, is not something to brag about. It's like taking out the garbage, it might be necessary, but it should not be a source of pride. How you act after a shooting goes a long way to show your reasonableness.

Chapter 6

Choosing a Gun

Preparing to buy your first handgun can be quite daunting. Handguns aren't cheap. New handguns range in price from $250.00 to $2,500.00. And to complicate the matter even further, there are many different manufacturers and choices. I tell people in my carry permit course that there are as many different types of handguns as the manufacturers can talk people into buying.

What is probably most confusing to someone new to this field is the fact that, for every make and model of handgun, there are three gun magazine writers telling their readers that their particular brand or caliber or gizmo is the best, and four others saying that the gun in question will get the reader killed.

I am often asked my opinion about Glock pistols. I usually say that what I think doesn't matter; it isn't my money or my safety on the line. My preference does not matter in your decision to buy your gun. What is important is that the gun fires every time you pull the trigger. Luckily for us, almost any modern name brand pistol is able to live up to this standard.

My wife likes Glocks best; I feel the same about S&W revolvers. Our preferences differ. You knowing your gun, knowing why you chose it, and knowing how it fits your needs are what build pride in gun ownership. A firearm is just a tool.

Choose a tool that works with your needs, one you are comfortable with. You do not need a $2,000 custom 1911A1 .45-acp with another $2,000 of bolt-on accessories to launch a bullet. Since it is the bullet that does the work, all you need is a safe, reliable handgun that you are comfortable with.

The handgun is very well represented in the world of guns; people like buying and owning handguns. Because of this sales popularity, many different functions and characteristics of handguns are available. Comparing these characteristics is like comparing pickup trucks and cars. There are many brands of pickups (revolvers), but generally they are all basically the same. In the car (semi-autos) world, there are sedans, sports cars, wagons, convertibles, limousines, economy class, and luxury designs. You can buy a vehicle or a firearm based solely on an arbitrary reason such as looks, popularity, or what the marketing hype in a gun magazine tells you. You may also buy a tool such as this by deciding your needs and weighing your options.

How you use a handgun means much more to me than how the handgun looks. A defensive pistol has a different set of criteria than a pistol bought solely to satisfy a Walter Mitty fantasy.

Size Matters

Size might not matter in all instances, but in the world of defensive handguns, size does matter. The size of both the handgun and the round are important. Rather than make cool-sounding platitudes about particular calibers, let's go through the benefits and drawbacks of different sizes.

One of the reasons that size matters in the firearm is that the larger the firearm, the easier it is to control recoil. Recoil is the movement of the gun in response to the round leaving the barrel. Recoil is caused by the law of physics, which states that for every action there is an equal and opposite reaction. There was a controlled explosion in the bowels of this piece of steel in your hand; thousands of pounds of pressure just pushed a bullet out the muzzle at supersonic speeds. There has to be some movement on the opposite end of the handgun. This is recoil. There is less felt recoil in a larger handgun because the weight of the handgun counteracts the recoil effects. Just as it is easier to push a little red wagon than a little red pickup truck, recoil moves a tiny handgun more than a huge "hand-cannon." The amount of recoil changes depending on the ammunition, also, so a small gun with a tiny round may recoil less than a big gun with a big round.

Length of the barrel also matters, as there are differences in the distance between the front and rear sights. This distance is called sight radius. A longer sight radius allows aiming mistakes to result in smaller targeting errors. Figure 6.01 shows a graphical representation of this. In both images, the distance from the rear sight to the target is the same. In the longer barreled firearm, the aiming error moves the round only a small distance off target, while the same error in the short barrel firearm causes a greater targeting error.

Imagine you were trying to navigate with a compass. Imagine you misread the compass by a degree. If you were only going a couple feet, your error would barely be noticed. But if you were going a couple miles you could be off hundreds of feet.

Rifles are not inherently more accurate than handguns just because of the length of the barrel (even though that does affect accuracy); they are more accurate because the greater sight radius reduces horizontal errors.

It is easy to be accurate with a firearm close up, being able to shoot targets where you can cover up all the holes with a single quarter becomes progressively harder the greater the distance to the target. If the fundamentals of firing are adhered to, and you shoot consistently, why is it that the size of your shot group grows larger with distance?

Think of the relationship between the firearm and your sights as a triangle, with one leg being the axis of the bore (Where the gun is being mechanically aimed and where the bullet will go), and the other leg representing where you think the firearm is aimed by using the sights. If you visualize this, you will notice that while the angle of the triangle stays the same, as the triangle grows in size the base gets larger. This makes your group size grow. As Mel Gibson's character said The Patriot, "Aim small, miss small."

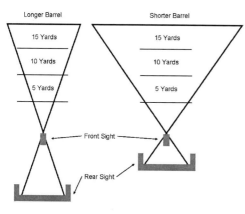

Figure 6.01
The Distance Between the Front and Rear Sights Can Affect Aiming Mistakes

If you take this idea and invert it by turning your mental triangle into an "X", you will see that the farther the base of the X is from the center the wider the ends are. This is important because it is hard for most people to judge distances with their eyes alone. Your sights may look to be lined up equally, but they may not be. By having a longer barrel, the front and rear sight are farther apart. This makes those small aiming errors more apparent to the shooter, just as those errors are more noticeable the farther the target is from the gun.

This concept is also illustrated when you're at the range and are able to shoot tiny groups at the three-yard target, but using the exact same techniques shoot a much larger pattern at the 25-yard target.

Barrel length also affects velocity of the round as it is fired. Ammunition works by burning gunpowder to create gas, and different powders have different burn rates. Its very easy for a discussion about how this works to become very technical, especially for someone that reloads their own ammunition, but at this point, all you need to know is that when you fire the same brand of ammunition in two firearms of the same caliber, the firearm with the longer barrel will generally have its bullet exit the barrel with more velocity and less muzzle flash than a shorter barreled firearm. More velocity means less drop of the bullet over distance, and more power when it hits the target.

Size can also be a drawback; a handgun can be too big. If your handgun is too large for your hands, accuracy suffers. A large handgun is harder to conceal. A large handgun may be uncomfortable to carry. This may make you less likely to carry it.

A good rule of thumb is to choose as much gun as you will carry and can control.

Ammunition size is also important. No matter how fancy the gun, you must be aware that the firearm is only the launching pad for the bullet. The bullet does the work. Cape Canaveral is a nice place to visit, but people go there to see the shuttle, not the launching pad.

All things being equal, large ammunition is more effective than small ammunition. Some very famous firearm instructors have made statements such as, "You can carry any caliber you want as long as it starts with a 4" or "a .380 is a good gun to carry when you don't feel like carrying a gun."

I agree with them. I think that anything under a .45 is minor, and anything under a .38 special is marginal; I normally carry a .380. I am aware of the shortcomings of my normal carry gun, but I balance this with the likelihood of an attack, the concealment issues I face, the convenience of carrying a smaller gun, and the fact that my wife carries a *much* larger gun. I also must say for those guys that may get any ideas, I am under no illusion that, should the excrement hit the oscillating air current generator, she would give me her gun to use.

Large calibers have more recoil; I like the .45 ACP round, and I used to carry a small 1911 .45; however, my arthritis will not let me practice with this gun as much as I should. The large bullet and light gun make it almost punishing for me to shoot for extended periods. This is relative to the person, as I know many who love to shoot a firearm that size. My larger Glock in a smaller caliber is fun for me to shoot because recoil is negligible. You must balance these factors when you decide to buy a firearm. This is a reason you should try to fire a gun before you buy it.

Handguns are defensive weapons; they do not contain anywhere near the power of rifles or shotguns. No matter what the caliber or size of the handgun, they are not able to provide a guarantee of the miracle "one shot stop." What a handgun does provide is the ability to conveniently have protection on your person when you need it. Because you cannot carry a .308 battle rifle to the mall, and you may be able to carry a handgun, do not sacrifice this ability to carry by buying a handgun too large to control or too uncomfortable to carry. A handgun does not do any good in your safe if you are attacked on the street.

Caliber

We have mentioned caliber. Now let's talk about what caliber actually is. Caliber is the size of the inside of the gun's barrel. It is measured in hundredths of an inch (such as .38) or in millimeters (such a 9mm). Caliber is measured across the diameter of the inside of the barrel.

With modern firearms, the caliber is stamped alongside the barrel and it should always match the ammunition you are attempting to fire with the handgun.

Types of Guns

Although both revolvers and semi-automatics have good and bad aspects, they both do the job you make them do.

Contrary to what gun stores, shows, and magazines say, the gun is not the most important piece of equipment. The brain behind the gun is. Now, that being said, let's discuss the benefits and drawbacks of the two main types of handguns: revolvers and semi-automatics so that you can decide for yourself which type of firearm best solves your need.

Revolvers

Revolvers are a type of pistol with a rotating cylinder containing a number of firing chambers. They typically hold 5 or 6 rounds, or bullets, each held in its own firing chamber. Revolvers are generally cheaper to purchase than semi-automatics, with a new revolver from a major manufacturer such as Taurus or Rossi being in the neighborhood of $350. The major benefits of this type of handgun include:

- They are easier to learn to manipulate, because there are generally fewer functions than with a typical semi-automatic.

- It is easier for weaker handed persons to operate, due to the lack of a slide. However, because of how a double action revolver operates, the trigger pull of a revolver can be heavier than a semi-automatic.

- Because the round is stationary, and does not move inside the firearm, you have more choice of ammunition.

- Because of fewer moving parts they are said to be more reliable.

- Also, because of the fewer moving parts, they are not as training intensive as a semi-automatic pistol (more about this later). However, this ease of use applies to the shooting of the handgun only. Loading a revolver under duress or at speed is more difficult than loading a typical semi-auto. At one end of the training spectrum, they are considered "beginner's guns"; but taken to mastery, they are the firearm of experts.

I prefer revolvers for home defense, as a home protection weapon will be stored loaded for an extended period of time. I prefer revolvers for this function because they have fewer moving parts, which in turn makes them less sensitive to a lack of cleaning and maintenance than semi-automatics. I also recommend revolvers for someone who is not going to train as intensively as recommended because this type of handgun has fewer functions to remember. In order to use a revolver, one only has to operate the trigger and the cylinder release; whereas a semi-automatic pistol generally has a trigger, a magazine release, a slide lock, and at least one safety lever.

Revolvers do have disadvantages, and it is because of these that police departments around the county have changed to semi-automatics. These disadvantages should be understood if the reader wishes to make a decision; therefore, I list them below:

Because single rounds are loaded individually into the cylinder, they can be slower to reload than the typical semi-automatic.

Due to width of the cylinder they are harder to conceal.

They don't carry as many rounds as a similar sized semi-automatic (5–6 rounds compared to 8 or 10 rounds in a semi-automatic).

Because a revolver contains separate chambers for each round, to fully load a revolver, the operator must put a round in each chamber (6 actions for 6 rounds). To fully load a semi-automatic, the operator has to insert a single loaded magazine into the pistol (one action for multiple rounds).

Figure 6.02
Common Double Action Revolver

Semi-Autos

Semi-automatic pistols fire a single cartridge or bullet each time the trigger is pressed. The pistol automatically extracts the spent casing and prepares to fire another round. A semi-automatic is sometimes called automatic, but the difference is that a true automatic can fire multiple rounds per trigger press. This seemingly small difference can cause tens of thousands of dollars in fines and years of time in federal penitentiaries, so be sure to know the difference.

A semi-automatic holds its rounds in a single device called a magazine (it is possible to offend some hard-line gun enthusiasts by calling a magazine a clip). This magazine is normally inserted into the grip of the handgun. These are the most popular handguns, and they are popular for many reasons.

Figure 6.03
Semi-Automatic Pistol

Some of the most recognized reasons are:

- It holds many rounds compared to a revolver. Normally a semi-auto magazine holds 8 to 10 rounds, but there are magazines capable of holding 15, 30, or even 100 rounds.

- It is easier to reload faster with a semi-automatic. This is because you only have to deal with magazines rather than many single cartridges.

- Due to popularity, there is a wider choice of accessories such as holsters available.

- It is easier to carry spare ammunition via pre-loaded magazines.

- They are easier to conceal due to thinner profile. There is no wide cylinder to bulge.

It is due to the amount of rounds easily carried in magazines on one's body and the amount of rounds in the pistol that caused the semi-automatic to replace the revolver in the arming of our nation's police. What has kept semi-automatics as the handgun of choice are the different features that are possible. A police force or a private user can decide the type of safety devices or modes of operation that they want in a firearm and buy a brand that has those features. Although this is a benefit, it also can become a drawback.

The possible drawbacks are:

- Semi-automatics are very training intensive. Before one begins to carry a semi-automatic for self-defense, it is recommended that the user fire 2 or 3 thousand rounds of the type of ammunition he or she intends to carry in the firearm to fully understand the function of the firearm.

- They have a complex action because of more moving parts. This translates to there being more chances for something to fail. While modern firearms and ammunition can fire thousands of rounds without malfunction, malfunctions can and do happen.

- Semi-automatics tend to be more expensive than a revolver.

- Because of the slide spring, it can be harder for people suffering from arthritis or of weaker stature to manipulate the slide; however, proper training can help with this. I have found from personal experience with new shooters that proper technique for racking the slide is more important that hand strength.

- They are more sensitive to ammunition type. Some types of semi-automatics are more prone to jam with certain types of ammunition. In a semi-automatic, the actual round is part of the mechanism, and moves inside the gun during the firing cycle. Very flat-nosed bullets or what is known as aggressive hollow-point bullets may actually jam against the ramp that feeds the round into the barrel of the handgun. For this reason, it is suggested that you train with the type of ammunition you intend to carry.

Other Types of Handguns

There are other types of handguns such as derringers, pepperboxes, or single-shot pistols. These are not recommended due to the limited ammunition capability, lack or limited sights they normally contain, or the difficulty in manipulation because of the extremely small size.

Chapter 7

Operating a Handgun

How Firearms Work

Firearms, no matter what type, are basically pretty simple. They all have certain parts. All firearms have a frame, a barrel, and an action. As stated before, firearms are just launching pads for bullets. They contain the bullet in the moment of firing and, using a barrel, direct the bullet toward its desired direction.

Frame

The frame is the structure to which all other components are attached. The grips are attached to the lower part of the frame. Grips are usually constructed of wood, rubber, or plastic. The grips are attached to the portion of the frame called the backstrap. On some guns, such as polymer-framed guns, there is not an actual backstrap that the grips attach to, however, we still use the term for reference purposes to cut down on confusion when we discuss things like the grip of the handgun.

The frame contains the trigger guard, which protects the trigger from being snagged causing an unintentional discharge. The rear sight is also attached to the frame, and is used in conjunction with the front sight post to aim the handgun.

Barrel

The barrel is the metal tube that the bullet passes through as it leaves the gun. The barrel contains a bore. The bore is the name for the inside of the barrel. Machined into the bore are grooves called rifling. This spiral machining inside the barrel puts spin on the bullet to stabilize it in flight. This is similar to a child's top. As long as the toy is spinning the top is stable and upright. When it slows down or stops spinning, the top is wobbly, erratic, and falls sideways. We don't want your fired bullet to move in a wobbly, erratic, or sideways movement.

A bullet without spin is inaccurate and may impact the target sideways, causing a keyhole-like puncture in the target. The rifling that causes the bullet to spin is made of two parts. Lands are the high spots of the rifling. Grooves are low spots or troughs in the rifling. This is important to know because this is how the caliber is measured.

Caliber is the size of the inside of the barrel. The caliber is measured in hundredths of an inch (such as .38) or in millimeters (such a 9mm). Caliber is measured from land to land, i.e., from high spot to high spot, across the diameter of the inside of the barrel.

Action

The action consists of the moving parts used to load, fire, and unload the firearm. Most of the moving parts of a handgun make up the action. The trigger, hammer, firing pin, slides on a semi-auto, or cylinder of a revolver are all parts of the action. Unlike the frame or the barrel the action is a group of parts and not a single piece.

How Bullets Work in the Firearm

I have said repeatedly that what is important is the bullet and not the firearm, so for the next couple minutes we are going to talk about how bullets actually work.

There are many terms used interchangeably when discussing rounds. Sometimes they are called rounds, bullets, cartridges, or ammunition. Each of these means something a little different, but for our purposes we will just discuss the component parts of a round of ammunition.

A cartridge is the complete, ready to use ammunition. It is what is loaded into the firearm to make it work.

A cartridge is made up of component parts:

The cartridge case is a brass, steel, aluminum, or other metal cup that holds all the other parts. It can be thought as the frame for the round. The base of the case is called the head, and the head is marked with a stamp that shows what caliber the case is designed for and who made it. The head also contains the primer.

There are two main types of priming systems for ammunition depending on what firearm you are shooting and how the cartridge is initiated.

A centerfire primer is a small cup containing a small amount of pressure sensitive explosive and a small anvil for the compound to be crushed against. When the firing pin strikes the primer held in the center of the cartridge head, the priming compound is crushed between the primer cup and the anvil causing a small detonation. This causes a flame to flare inside the cartridge case igniting the propellant.

In a rimfire case, there is no central primer; the priming compound is mechanically spun in the base of the case itself, so that when a firing pin strikes the rim of the case it causes the flame to be created.

Most centerfire ammunition can be taken apart with special tools and reloaded to be used again. It is outside the capabilities of the hobbyist to reload rimfire ammunition.

The most common in terms of calibers available is centerfire. Almost every firearm suitable for defensive use will be centerfire. Rimfire is more common in terms of quantity as it's much smaller and cheaper. The .22 is the most common rimfire cartridge and sees much use as a target or practice round.

Inside the case is a propellant of some type. Modern ammunition contains smokeless gunpowder that when ignited by the primer rapidly burns creating a large volume of gas very quickly. It is the increase in pressure caused by this gas that propels the bullet out of the barrel at high speed.

The mouth of the cartridge case is pressed around the bullet. When the round is ignited by the primer, the mouth of the cartridge case flares out slightly, creating a seal inside the firing chamber. This seal does not allow the hot gasses to flow anywhere but down the barrel, which is the main reason it's not safe to use rounds not specifically made in the caliber of the handgun.

There are many types of bullets, from inexpensive cast lead bullets for target practice to specially designed bullets with an indention in the head that is designed to expand inside the target. Any bullet fired from a handgun faces a limitation in energy because of simple physics. Any round powerful enough to pick up the target and throw it across the room would pick up the shooter and throw them across the room at the same time. A hollow point bullet is designed to maximize the release of its energy inside the target by rapidly opening up in size and staying inside the target rather than passing completely through them and possibly hitting and innocent bystander to the rear.

When a firearm is loaded and ready to fire, the trigger is pressed. This causes a firing pin to strike the back of the round or bullet at the primer. This primer contains a very small amount of a pressure-sensitive explosive, which is ignited by the slamming of the firing pin into the primer causing a hot flash of fire inside the bullet.

Once the gun is fired and the bullet leaves the barrel, the inertia caused by the fast-moving bullet causes force to be applied in the opposite direction of the bullet's travel. This opposite movement is recoil. Recoil is generally not very severe and is mitigated by bullet size, handgun size, type of handgun action, and the body mechanics of the person shooting. As I have said before, larger bullets have more energy therefore more recoil, but larger handguns absorb recoil and reduce it. Also, firearm design and how you hold the handgun also has an effect on the recoil you feel as you fire the handgun.

The Mechanics of Revolvers

We have discussed previously that revolvers got their name from the revolving cylinder that contains multiple firing chambers. We did not discuss what a firing chamber is at that point, but we will now. A firing chamber is the location the round or bullet is in when it fires. Because a round in a revolver fires from its position in the cylinder, each position in the revolver's cylinder is considered a firing chamber.

After you load the cylinder, close it, and pull the trigger, a few things will happen. In a double action revolver (the only kind of revolver you should use for self-defense), the cylinder will rotate to place a firing chamber in line with the barrel. Simultaneously, the hammer will move rearward cocking the handgun.

The revolver is timed so that when the trigger is fully to the rear, the firing chamber is lined up with the barrel, and the hammer is released from its rearmost or cocked position.

The hammer then falls and either a firing pin attached to the hammer strikes the bullet's primer, or the hammer strikes an internal firing pin inside the revolver. Either way, the hammer falling causes the cartridge to ignite.

The Mechanics of Semi-Autos

This type of handgun is more complicated than revolvers, as the round is not stationary inside the pistol like it is in the revolver. The rounds are loaded into a removable magazine. This magazine is spring loaded, and as a cartridge or round is removed from the magazine into the gun, another moves up to replace it.

When a magazine is inserted into a semi-automatic pistol, the bottom of the pistol's closed slide puts pressure on the top of the magazine. This pressure pushes the rounds slightly lower than the spring pressure from the magazine wants the rounds to sit. As the slide is pulled back, this release of pressure pushes a round upward so that when the slide moves forward it catches on the tip of the extended round and push it forward. As the round moves forward it butts against a feed ramp. This ramp is attached to the barrel and guides the round into the barrel. Because the round is fired while inside the barrel, the internal end of the barrel is also the pistol's firing chamber.

This slide movement to the rear also cocks the hammer on most models of semi-autos. Some semi-automatics are called Double-Action Only (DAO). A DAO pistol has a disconnector that does not allow the hammer to stay cocked (held to the rear); each trigger pull cocks the hammer just like a double action revolver.

Either way, once a round is inside the pistol's chamber and the handgun is cocked, the trigger can be pressed to the rear, releasing the hammer to strike the pistol's firing pin. This in turn strikes the primer and ignites the round.

Semi-automatics then use the power of the round's inertia to push the slide to the rear. A small hook called an extractor clips itself to the rim at the base of the spent round and pulls it from the firing chamber. Once the round is hooked and the slide is fully to the rear, an additional small bar called an ejector is exposed from the face of the slide. This ejector pushes the round off the extractor and out and away from the gun.

Figure 8.01
Extractor

Figure 8.02
Ejector

The slide is then pulled forward under spring pressure, picking up another round and preparing the cycle to begin again. What is nice about a semi-automatic handgun is that all this is done automatically by the mechanics inside the pistol. Each trigger pull by the shooter not only fires a single round, but as long as there are rounds in the magazine, the semi-automatic will prepare itself to fire another round at the next trigger pull.

Clearing (Unloading) Procedures

Clearing is the process of unloading a firearm. It is a procedure that should be performed anytime a firearm is handled. It is generally impossible to tell if a firearm is unloaded just by looking at it.

There are different procedures for clearing revolvers and semi-automatics; however, the principles are the same.

Clearing Revolvers

If a revolver is going to be handled, pick it up in your dominant hand by the grips. With your thumb, push the cylinder release lever. This lever (or button) is located on the left side of the pistol. Using your support hand, push the cylinder open and visually inspect the cylinder to ensure that no rounds are present.

If you see rounds present, raise the barrel of the pistol straight up keeping the pistol between chest and waist level. Use the palm of your support hand to firmly press the ejector rod located on the muzzle end of the cylinder. Pushing this rod down toward the cylinder will push out any rounds. Once this is done, lower the barrel and inspect the cylinder again. At no time should your trigger finger be inside the trigger guard. You also need to be careful as you do this not to muzzle your support hand as you move it around the barrel. Even though you are unloading the handgun, you still need to be aware that you're pointing the muzzle in a safe direction.

If the rounds inside the cylinder are unfired, they will fall free as soon as you raise the barrel; however, if they have been fired, you will need to press the ejector rod to push out the empty cases. This is because the mouth of the round was flared out to create that seal we talked about earlier.

When you are on the range you're going to be tempted to dump these expended cases into your hand. Do not do it. When you do anything but let them fall to the ground you are training yourself to dump your empty casings in your hand. It will slow you down in a crisis situation. I can understand that on the range it is extra work to pick up the spent cases from the ground after you are finished, but time has shown that, under stress, you

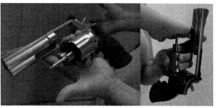

Figure 8.03
Unloading a Revolver Is Simple

perform the actions you have practiced. Actual gunfights have resulted in dead policemen with unloaded guns and spent cases in their pockets.

In a fight you do not rise to the situation, you default to the level you have mastered. So *always* practice in the manner you intend to use your handgun.

Clearing Semi-Autos

The very first thing that should be done when clearing a semi-automatic is that the magazine should be removed. The magazine release is generally located behind the trigger on the grip or at the bottom of the grip near the floorplate of the magazine. Removing the magazine removes all rounds except the one in the chamber. Remembering how a semi-auto works, if a round is removed from the chamber with rounds in the magazine, the slide will automatically pick up a new round and reload the chamber.

Failing to remove the magazine *first* is a major cause of handgun accidents. Many negligent discharges have occurred because the user removed the round from the chamber before removing the magazine, then removed the magazine leaving one round still in the handgun.

Once the magazine has been removed, grasp the handgun in your dominant hand as if you were going to use it. Then, with fingers off the trigger, using the support hand to grasp the rear of the slide, and keeping the pistol pointed in a safe direction, pull the slide to the rear and either lock it back or hold it open.

With the slide to the rear, visually inspect the chamber and, if the slide is able to be locked to the rear, physically inspect the chamber by sticking your little finger into it. This ensures that it is in fact empty and you did not just "go through the motions." If you have ever moved and then driven to your old house on auto-pilot, you understand that sometimes we get used to doing things a certain way. If you have cleared your handgun hundreds of times and never saw a round in the chamber, you can fool your brain so that the one time there is a round in the chamber it doesn't see it. That's why we physically check.

There's no fooling the finger.

Giving the Handgun to Another Person

There is etiquette that has evolved to ensure the safety of others around handguns. If you are clearing the handgun to either give it to another person or to demonstrate using it, you should show the empty chambers to the other person. It is polite to give the handgun to the other person grips first, so that they can take the handgun from you by the grips. Do so with the action open or the cylinder swung out on a revolver.

Never point a handgun, either loaded or unloaded, at another person unless you are justified legally to shoot that person.

Loading Procedures

As with clearing a firearm, the procedures for loading change depending on handgun type. Always read your manual before you use your firearm for the first time.

Revolver Loading

Loading revolvers is simple. Once you have cleared the revolver, and with the barrel pointed at the ground, place a single round in each firing chamber. While this is simple, it is also slow. If you remember the earlier section on revolvers, the slowness to load is the main reason police agencies went to semi-automatics.

To reduce the movements it takes to load a revolver (to increase speed), various speed loading devices have been created. There are two basic types, the speed strip and the speed loader.

A speed strip is a rubber bar with cutouts for six rounds. Using a speed strip allows the loading of two rounds at a time

Figure 8.04
Using a Speed Strip

instead of one. This cuts the loading movements in half. It also allows for easier carrying of spare ammunition, as it keeps the rounds together.

The second type is the speed loader. A speed loader is a device

that is shaped to match the chambers of the model of revolver for which it is made. Rounds are held by their rims by a pin inside the speed loader. The speed loader is then lined up with the cylinder, allowing all chambers to be filled at the same time. This can be extremely fast if practiced.

It is not necessary to load the entire cylinder to fire the weapon. Police have been found killed with partially loaded cylinders while in the process of reloading. Your revolver will fire as long as there is a live round inline with the barrel (top cylinder) when the hammer falls.

Figure 8.05
Using a Speed Loader

The problem is that, as the hammer is drawn back, the cylinder rotates. If a less than a full cylinder is loaded with ammunition you must ensure that the cylinder immediately behind the barrel is empty. You must also ensure that the first loaded round is directly next to the top cylinder in the opposite direction of rotation. This means that, if the cylinder rotates clockwise, the loaded round must be to the left of the top cylinder and, if the cylinder rotates counterclockwise, the loaded round must be to the right of the top cylinder.

Because of this detail, it is important to become familiar with the rotation of your handgun cylinder. Luckily, this will not change in your handgun, and most firearms rotate clockwise. There are a few, such as Colt, that rotate counterclockwise.

Loading Semi-Automatics

Loading a semi-automatic involves inserting a loaded magazine and placing a round inside the chamber. There are two ways to do this: administrative loading and reloading from a locked open slide.

Administrative Load

With the administrative load, you're either on the range or preparing to carry. There is no time constraint placed on you. Pick up the handgun in your dominant hand. Pick up a loaded magazine in your support hand. Place your index finger along the edge of the magazine on the bullet side of the magazine, with the flat head end of the round against your palm. Raise the handgun to eye level and while keeping the handgun pointed in a safe direction insert the magazine into the base of the gun. Use your support hand index finger on the magazine to help your brain find the magazine well. This works because your brain keeps track of its parts, otherwise you'd stab your eye instead of your mouth when eating spaghetti. Once the magazine is inserted, use the palm of your support hand to fully seat the magazine. You want to hear a "click." If the magazine does not fully snap into the gun then the slide will not be able to pick up rounds, therefore causing a malfunction.

Figure 8.06
Finger Indexed on Magazine
for a Non-Visual Clue

Once the magazine is in place, you need to chamber a round. This can be difficult for the first time shooter, because he or she may try to muscle the slide instead of using proper technique. While keeping the handgun pointed in a safe direction (meaning not to your side) grasp the top of the slide behind the ejection port with your support hand. While pushing forward on the handgun grip with your dominant hand; pull straight back on the slide with your support hand. Do this firmly, you're not going to break the gun. When the slide is moved as far as it will mechanically move, release the slide with your support hand and let the slide "sling-shot" forward.

Do not attempt to assist or help the slide go forward. To do so will only keep the firearm from functioning as designed and may cause a feeding malfunction. This is a good example of where you need to decide what to do and then do it. Hesitation, or a stop-and-go approach will cause you to only half rack the slide. It is not

Figure 8.07
Proper Grip on the Slide
to Pull the Slide to the Rear

under extreme pressure, but there is a spring you have to

compress. The failure to fully pull the slide to the rear and release it in a single motion can cause malfunctions such as a double feed or failure to load. Do not let this frustrate you. I have never had a student that had trouble racking the slide the first time have trouble racking the slide once they began using proper technique and using that technique decisively.

Slide Lock Reload

You may need to load the gun after firing it dry. Most defensive firearms have a feature that will cause the slide to lock open when the magazine is empty. If your firearm does not do this, then simply reload it using the previous technique.

If your slide locks open on an empty magazine, then slightly invert and turn the muzzle about 45 degrees inboard, which means that the barrel should still be pointed downrange, but slightly to the left if you're holding the pistol in your right hand. This movement causes the gun to slide slightly in your hand so that the magazine release (if it's located behind and below the trigger as is normal) is now under the thumb of your shooting hand.

You should simultaneously reach for your loaded magazine with your support hand. Index your finger on the front of the new magazine just as with the administrative load. Once you have the loaded magazine in your hand, use the thumb of your shooting hand to release the empty magazine. Let it fall free just as you would empty cases from a revolver.

Your gun should be at eye level and your focus should be on your target. You do not want to be fumbling and looking at your magazines and let your attacker have the opportunity to hide out of sight. Slide your new magazine inside the handgun just as before. Once it locks in place, you can release the slide and your gun will once again be fully loaded.

Some firearms have a release on the slide that will send it forward; however, it's a lot easier under stress to reach up and grasp the back of the slide with your support hand, just as you did to rack it, and pull the slide slightly to the rear. Once you have moved the slide backward slightly, the slide lock will be released and you can let the slide go and it will sling shot forward just as it did administratively.

Done correctly, and with practice, this is a very quick method to reload and can be done without having to take your eyes off of your threat.

Some things to be aware of:

- If you are reloading during a fight, do so behind cover. You do not want to be standing in the middle of the street cursing your empty gun while bullets are coming at you.
- Never take your eyes off the threat. You don't want him to sneak away and come at you from a blind spot while you are reloading.
- Never drop your magazine until you have a full one in your hand. Sometimes people reload their gun without fully emptying the magazine. But some guns are designed not to work without a magazine in the handgun even if there is a round in the chamber. If you have such a gun, and drop your magazine, but your spare somehow gets lost, your gun is worthless. It has happened, just don't let it happen to you.
- Do not try to reload at warp speed. If you try to move faster than your training you only cause yourself to fumble. Try for smooth. Going slow enough to make sure you only have to do it once is many times faster than fumbling at speed.
- Keep movements to a minimum. Keep the gun at eye level and near the same extension you use to shoot. Bringing the gun down to your waist is natural, but it makes you look down, and takes time to get the gun back unto position.

Safeties

A safety is a mechanical device on a firearm intended to prevent the weapon from discharging. There are numerous types of safeties, both internal and external.

Revolvers generally do not have any external safeties; however, new revolvers might have a lock built into them that will render the hammer unable to be cocked. Modern revolvers also have a hammer block, which protects the primer in the top cylinder from being impacted by the firing pin unless the trigger is pulled.

Semi-automatics have a much wider variety of safeties. Some have a grip safety that must be depressed by the firing hand for the weapon to fire. Various levers could be built into the handgun to lock the hammer and prevent the handgun from firing.

Some of these levers disconnect the trigger so that they must be turned on for the trigger to activate the firing pin. Others will safely release (or drop) the hammer without firing the handgun. This type of safety is known as a de-cocker. As you may imagine, the ability to de-cock a firearm that must be cocked to fire (such as a single action revolver or semi-auto) is an important safety feature.

A final safety device on some semi-automatic handguns is a magazine disconnect. In firearms with this type of safety, the handgun cannot fire if the magazine is removed. The idea behind this is that, in the event of an assault, the handgun owner may remove or drop the magazine so that the attacker cannot use the gun if the attacker is able to take it away from the owner.

No matter what type of safety the handgun has, it is no good if you cannot use it under stress. Finally, know that all safeties are mechanical devices and are prone to failure. Never use the safety as a crutch and expect it to protect you from unsafe handling procedures.

Malfunctions

There are two types of malfunction—ammunition and weapon. In this modern age, both can be reduced to near 100% function levels by purchasing quality equipment and then giving your equipment proper care.

One of the reasons to fire many hundreds of rounds of practice ammunition in your self-defense handgun is to ensure that it is 100% reliable. I can tolerate a supremely accurate gun that is so finely machined with tolerances so tight that a grain of sand or grit causes it to malfunction a time or two every couple hundred rounds if it's a target gun. But on a gun that I depend on to save my life I do not tolerate any malfunctions. I ensure that my defense gun and defense ammunition work together flawlessly.

Ammunition Malfunctions

Malfunctions of ammunition are rare when using quality factory ammunition; however, they do happen. On a range, there are specific administrative practices to increase safety that would be ignored if the same malfunction occurred in a lethal force situation.

As we discuss these practices hopefully it will be clear why this is one of the only areas that you train differently than you would desire to act in an actual hostile shooting incident.

Misfire

A misfire is a failure of the round to fire after the primer has been struck, which is the most common type of malfunction. Its causes are many: Reloaded ammunition with poor primers, a broken firing pin, or a firing pin that does not strike the primer deep enough to ignite the cartridge are common causes. Another overlooked cause is using WD-40 or some other non-gun cleaner when cleaning your gun. Cleaners such as these are notorious for finding a way into the ammunition and deactivating the primer compound.

Hangfire

A perceptible delay in ignition of the cartridge after the primer was struck is known as a hangfire. When you have a hangfire, you pull the trigger, and nothing happens, just like a misfire; however, after a noticeable delay the round will fire. This can be devastating if a hangfire is thought to be a misfire and the round is ejected before it goes off.

When a cartridge fails to fire immediately, it will not be known if it is a hangfire or a misfire. Therefore, in a training situation, always act the safest way possible and treat them both as if it is a hangfire. To do this, keep the handgun pointed downrange, and wait at least 15 seconds before opening the action and removing the cartridge.

During a lethal force encounter, one must balance the dangers of misdiagnosing a hangfire with the danger of not returning fire. Obviously, when someone is trying to shoot you, he is more dangerous than the slight possibility of injury from a hangfire that may or may not exist. In a lethal force scenario, if your handgun fails to fire, treat it as a misfire and perform the tap-rack-assess maneuver that we will discuss shortly.

Squib Load

A squib load is when less than normal pressure is developed after the ignition of the cartridge. A squib load is indicated by reduced noise or recoil. Keep the handgun pointed down range and unload. Check the chamber and barrel for obstructions.

The danger with a squib load is that the bullet becomes stuck in the barrel. If another round is fired, causing the second bullet to impact the first bullet inside the barrel, a huge increase in pressure inside the barrel results. This pressure could be enough to cause the barrel to explode. I don't want that to happen when it is in my hand, and I am sure you feel the same way.

A squib load is commonly diagnosed by a "pop without a bang" when firing. Just remember, if your firing your handgun and you see, feel, or hear anything that is not normal, stop firing and check your handgun for any defects.

Handgun Malfunctions

Malfunctions happen; that's why we learn how to deal with them. In the worst-case scenario of a lethal force situation, do not allow a weapon malfunction to cost you your life. Maintain your handgun regularly, inspect it before use, fire enough ammunition to learn what brand of ammunition works best in your handgun, and practice how to fix malfunctions.

Figure 8.08
The Obstruction in
the Center of the
Barrel Is a Bullet

Revolvers

A malfunction in a double action revolver is generally easy to resolve. If the gun fails to fire, pull the trigger again. Keep pulling the trigger until the handgun fires, or you have attempted to shoot it as many times as the revolver has chambers. Once you have attempted this, dump the rounds and reload.

Semi-automatics

These are a little more complicated, as the round is part of the firing mechanism and moves in the course of loading, firing, extracting, and ejecting.

Failure to Fire

Click, no bang; your weapon is loaded, but nothing happened. It could be a misfire, or it could be a magazine that is not fully seated. Either way, there is a simple universal first step in attempting to fix the problem.

Tap – Rack – Assess

Tap the bottom of the magazine to insure the magazine is fully seated in the handgun.

Rack the slide sharply to the rear by grasping it firmly and pulling it backward. Then once it is fully to the rear, let it go to allow it to slingshot forward. This will remove the malfunctioning round and load a fresh cartridge into the barrel of the handgun.

Assess the situation and determine if a shot needs to be fired. The military teaches this as tap-rack-bang, and trains its members to fire a round after racking the slide; however, the armed citizen never has the luxury of firing a shot without consideration as to where the bullet will go.

Stovepipe

A stovepipe malfunction is a partially ejected bullet case that binds the slide and does not allow the slide to fully close (go into battery). A portion of the spent casing will protrude from the slide much like a stovepipe protrudes from a wood stove.

Figure 8.09
Stovepipe

Remedial action is simple. Forcefully rake your support hand across the top of the slide from the front of the gun to the rear. The purpose of this action is to catch and push the protruding round out and away from the handgun. Do this while pointing the handgun downrange, and ensure that the muzzle never points at your support hand.

Once the round is knocked clear, rack the slide to the rear to feed a new round and assess the situation.

Double Feed

This is an intensive malfunction that takes some work to correct. This malfunction is caused when, for what-ever reason, a round is not extracted from the barrel of the firearm and another round is picked up by the slide and stuck inside the handgun.

Figure 8.10
Double Feed

To clear this malfunction, the first thing needed is to lock the slide to the rear if the firearm has a slide lock. If the firearm does not have a slide lock, move on to the next step, which is to remove the magazine from the pistol.

This could be difficult and the magazine might need to be pried out with the fingers. After the magazine is removed, grasp the rear of the slide in the support hand and rapidly and positively rack the slide 3 or 4 times to clear the action. Then re-insert a loaded magazine. Charge the pistol (by racking the slide to insert another round into the chamber). Reassess the situation.

Cleaning

Handgun cleaning is often overlooked or disregarded. It can be thought of as a chore. It is sometimes thought to be unnecessary when the firearm operator owns a polymer handgun such as a Glock. This is not true. There are many reasons and times for cleaning your handgun. This is especially true if your handgun is to be used for defensive purposes. If you stake your life on a piece of equipment, do you not think that equipment deserves proper care?

When to Clean

Clean your handgun every time it is used. After each range session, disassemble your handgun and clean it. You should also clean your firearm before use if stored for long periods. Lastly, when you first purchase a new firearm, you should clean it before you use it for the first time.

I need to emphasize that before you begin to clean your handgun for the first time, read the manual. When I bought my first new Glock pistol, I immediately broke it down and cleaned it. I noticed copper grease on the slides and thought it was residue from the factory's test firing. It wasn't until after shooting my first 500 rounds that I bothered to read the manual. Once I did read the manual, I learned that this grease was a lapping compound that was designed to properly form the gun slide and frame rails to match each other, and was put there on purpose. I also learned that the manufacturer recommended that the gun not be cleaned until this residue was naturally removed by firing.

This shows that, no matter how experienced or knowledgeable you think you are, you never know everything. Always read the manual before handling a new firearm.

Why Clean

Correct cleaning helps ensure that handguns will operate properly. When the inside of the handgun is full of dirt, grime, carbon, rust, pocket lint, etc., the levers and springs cannot function properly. In some extreme cases, fouling of the barrel can even increase pressures inside the pistol to dangerous levels. Cleaning a handgun also allows a level of inspection that general use does not. When you are closely looking at the internal portions of your pistol to ensure your gun is clean, you can also see any broken pieces.

Cleaning preserves the finish and protects against rust. A handgun can be an expensive investment. It is common for new firearms to cost over $1,000. When you factor in that resale value is calculated partly by the amount of finish left on the gun, it makes sense to keep your gun free of rust. The natural oil on your hands alone can cause rust; it is important that you clean this off after you handle the firearm.

Lastly, and as importantly as any other reason, cleaning reinforces handgun use. Once you have cleaned your gun, you need to operate it without ammunition to ensure that it has been put back together properly. This manipulation of the handgun, without ammunition, will reinforce in your head the operations you need to take to properly use the weapon.

Cleaning Materials

Although it is usually easiest to buy your cleaning materials in kit form at a store, it is not necessary. A sporting goods store will normally carry the basic items needed to clean a handgun. These items are:

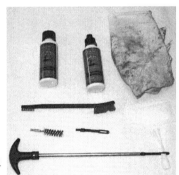

- Cloth patches
- Cleaning rod
- Soft cloth
- Cleaning rod attachments (screwed into end of rod)
- Bore brush
- Tip to hold patches
- Small brush (old toothbrush works fine)
- Bore cleaner
- Lubricant

Figure 8.11
Common Cleaning
Materials

When buying a kit, the label will designate whether the kit is for a rifle, a shotgun, or a pistol. It will also designate the calibers for which the kit is used. It is not necessary to purchase a new kit for each handgun you buy, as most parts are interchangeable. If you already have a pistol cleaning kit, and have a new gun in a different caliber, simply buy cleaning rod attachments (and maybe patches) for the new caliber.

How to Clean

- Be sure the gun is unloaded, action open, and no ammunition is present.

- Attach bore brush to rod and dip brush in bore cleaner.

- Run the soaked bore brush through the gun's bore several times.

- Remove bore brush and attach patch tip and patch, and dip the tip in bore cleaner.

- Run patch through bore of pistol barrel 10 to 12 times.

- Attach a clean patch in the patch tip and run it through the barrel several times.

- Inspect the patch; if it is dirty, repeat the above actions until the patch is clean.

- Run a lightly oiled patch through the bore.

- If cleaning a revolver, repeat the above for each chamber of the cylinder.

- Use the small brush, dipped in bore cleaner, to clean other areas.

- Wipe the outside of the pistol with a cloth and add a light coat of oil.

Lightly lubricate (lubrication points vary with each type of handgun). Ensure that you use the type of oil and lubrication points designated in the firearm's instruction manual. Too much or the wrong kind of oil can hurt performance. Too much oil will attract dirt and grime that can mix together to make an abrasive paste that wears your firearm or causes it to jam. The wrong kind of oil (like WD-40) can seep into your ammunition and cause ammunition malfunctions.

Once you have finished cleaning the handgun and re-assembled it, perform a function check of each operation of the pistol. This is performed before you reunite the pistol with its ammunition. Make sure everything works, including all the safeties and all the levers. Now is the time to locate any broken parts, not when your life hangs in the balance.

There have been accidents during cleaning when the shooter function checks the firearm a couple times, gets distracted, loads the gun, and then fires what he thinks is an empty firearm causing a very bad, very loud day. Anytime you are finished function checking or dry-firing your firearm, set it down and say *out loud* "I am done dry-firing my firearm." This may seem silly at first, but it creates a mental stop that may prevent a tragedy.

Chapter 8

Carrying a Gun

Open Carry vs. Concealed

As previously stated, not all states require a handgun to be concealed. As a proponent of the second amendment of the U.S. Constitution I applaud such laws, but I discourage the practice of open carry to my students for tactical reasons. However, where legal, there is nothing wrong with open carry, as long as it is done in a manner consistent with personal responsibility and good gun etiquette, because when you choose to carry your handgun in the open, you become a representative to all gun owners.

There are many reasons why instructors and state governments discourage open carry, some legal and some tactical. In today's society, many people are either uncomfortable or downright afraid of being around a firearm. Anytime we as armed citizens make those sheep scared of us, we erode our ability to continue to carry. If you carry a handgun in the open someone will most likely call the police. Police will come because of a "man with a gun" call. Being the recipient of such police attention is not something you would like to repeat.

Carrying a gun is a private choice, not something to be shared. This is not to say that you should be ashamed of carrying a gun or hide the gun. The opposite is true; the decision to take personal responsibility is admirable and something to be proud of. The reason you should keep this decision private is the same as the reason to carry concealed. You don't want people with low morals and an axe to grind to accuse you of "brandishing."

What do you think would happen if a scorned ex of yours called the police and said you threatened him or her with a gun and then described it and where you carried it? What would happen if the police then responded to find the exact same weapon in the location where it was described?

If the reasons above are not enough, I have another reason to prefer concealed carry—tactics. Criminals pick those they think they can beat. Criminals are not fair, nor do they take chances. If you carry a handgun in the open and are still attacked, rest assured that the criminal will give you no chance to get to your gun; it is more likely the criminal will kill you at the onset of the attack. It is also possible for criminals to take your open carry as a direct challenge and specifically target you.

Deadly force is a serious aspect of self-defense. It should never be used for anything other than an attack on an innocent life. You should never use deadly force to protect property. Sometimes it is wiser to let the street rat take your wallet, or give him your money rather than fight him. If your handgun is concealed, you have the choice to use it or to not use it. When your handgun is in the open, the attacker has all the choices. Does it not make sense to keep all the choices under your control, especially the option to either use or not use deadly force?

Holster Types

There are many types of holsters and many styles of manu-facture. Do not be caught in the attempt to save money and buy some "el-cheapo" holster; the first time your pistol falls out in the restroom of the local big-box store you will wish you bought a reputable holster. No matter what type of holster you use, your finger should not be placed in the trigger guard until the handgun is pointed at the target. Handguns should not be carried stuck in the waistband or in a pocket.

Anyone who carries a handgun for any length of time will end up with a box of holsters; this is because what looks good or feels nice in the store does not always stand up to daily use. To help reduce that waste of time, space, and money, let's discuss the main types of holsters and some pros and cons of each type.

Outside the Waistband (OWB) Holsters

These are types of holsters designed to be worn outside of clothing and attached to a belt. They are the most common type of holster and have many variations.

The most common of these are strong side carry holsters. This type of holster is worn on the dominant side hip, and is one of the fastest and most natural carry methods. A problem with this type of carry is the need for some type of "cover garment" like a coat.

A problem with strong side OWB holsters affects half of the carry populace. Most females generally have wider hips and shorter torsos than most men. OWB holsters worn on the strong side can push the butt of the handgun into a woman's side because of this natural curve. This makes it difficult for her to draw without contorting her upper body away from the handgun.

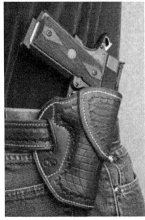

Figure 7.01
Strong-side OWB

Crossdraw holsters are worn with the holster on the wearer's support side (non-dominant side) with the butt of the gun facing toward the dominant side. When drawing a handgun carried in this manner the dominant hand reaches across the body. This can cause problems if the attacker attempts to either disarm you or prevent you from drawing. In this carry method, the handgun is easier to reach by someone facing you than it is by you. This method is useful for those who spend time driving. A weapon carried in this manner is easy to reach when seated and is one of the most comfortable for long periods of sitting.

A small of the back or SOB holster is worn in the middle of the wearer's back, right above the buttocks. A holster like this grants the wearer a large amount of concealment when worn with a cover garment. It is also very comfortable for someone who spends a large amount of time standing or moving. This holster's drawbacks become apparent when the user is seated. Not only are they uncomfortable to wear when seated, drawing the weapon from this position while seated is difficult if not impossible.

Figure 7.02
Crossdraw OWB

Figure 7.03
SOB OWB

Care must be taken when using a holster of this type to not point the weapon at your own body when drawing. Another issue that you must consider with an SOB holster is that, due to the location on your body, severe injury to your spine may occur if you are knocked to the ground. Many police agencies prohibit wearing equipment at the small of the back because of the risk of spinal injury. Secondly, in the event that you are knocked to the ground, it may be impossible for you to draw your weapon if your attacker is on top of you. However, an SOB carry is popular because it is very easy to conceal a handgun in this manner, and when not seated, it is very comfortable.

Inside the Waistband (IWB) Holsters

These holsters are worn at the belt-line like OWB holsters; however, they are worn inside the pants. These holsters generally allow the shirt to be tucked in over the holster, allowing a concealed carry without a cover garment. These holsters are a balance between concealment and speed. They are slower to draw from than an OWB holster, but are cooler to wear in the summer, as they do not require the use of a coat.

Figure 7.04
IWB Holster

A problem with IWB holsters comes from it being *inside* your waistband. The holster or firearm itself can rub against your skin, which can be uncomfortable, or allow sweat to discolor or possibly damage your handgun. This can be solved by wearing a t-shirt or other garment between your skin and the firearm.

Shoulder Holsters

There are two main types of shoulder holsters—vertical and horizontal. These describe the direction the barrel points in relation to the ground. A horizontal holster holds the gun with the barrel parallel to the ground. A horizontal shoulder holster is comfortable to wear, and easy to draw, but the handgun is

Figure 7.05
Horizontal Shoulder Holster

Figure 7.06
Vertical Shoulder
Holster

pointing at anyone directly behind the wearer. This is undesirable from a safety aspect, and very undesirable from a personal relations standpoint if the handgun is worn without a covering garment.

A vertically holstered gun has its barrel perpendicular to the ground. The muzzle points directly at the ground. This is usually a much better choice.

Whether the handgun is worn vertically or horizontally, many of the problems are the same. Namely, the handgun has the same retention and draw problems as the crossdraw holster, because the strong hand is reaching across the body. Another problem is that the gun can be difficult to re-holster. This is a problem after a use of force scenario, albeit a much smaller concern because you are always going to re-holster after the threat has passed. You also need to be aware that because a shoulder holster is worn between the body and the inside of the support side arm it's easy to point the handgun at your own body while drawing or re-holstering.

The "Belly Band" Holster

The belly band is a cloth, elastic, and Velcro band that is worn under a shirt. These holsters offer a deeper concealment option than conventional holsters. The problem with these holsters is that they can slip around and move under the shirt, irritate the skin, or if tightened enough to prevent slippage they can compress the body and be uncomfortable.

The belly band is designed to be worn against the skin, underneath the clothing; however, this can be very uncomfortable for some people.

Figure 7.07 "Belly Band"

Groin Holsters

These are like the belly band except they have a front pocket that drops down in the front of your underwear. They work well for concealment; however, some people find them uncomfortable. Others do not like them when they realize where the muzzle points.

Pocket Holsters

This type of holster is used for smaller guns carried in a pocket. They work particularly well for .380 caliber or smaller weapons. They prevent wear or damage to both the handgun and your clothing. Care should be taken to get a holster that breaks the outline of the handgun so that if seen, the outline looks more like a wallet and less like a gun.

The main problem with this type of holster is that when the handgun is drawn, the holster may be drawn with it. Special holsters are made with either a rubber strap to catch the pocket material or a tab to catch on the top of the pocket. Another problem is that you must teach yourself not to use this pocket for the carrying of coins, keys, or other materials.

Figure 7.08
Pocket Holster

Figure 7.09
Ankle Holster

Ankle Holsters

These are popular for backup guns. A family member of mine has carried a backup gun this way for decades without anyone ever knowing. I only found out when he unlimbered to follow the gun-free school zone law prior to visiting a school program. I remember being shocked that I did not know he carried in this manner.

The problem with this manner of carry is not concealment; it is access. A person with a "spare tire" might not be able to reach an ankle holster in an effective or efficient manner. You must also make sure that the cuffs of your pants are large enough to cover the handgun and not show its outline or "print." You must also be aware of the holster possibly showing when you sit down. I find this type of holster best for those with sedentary jobs, as it's easiest to draw from this type of holster while seated. It is nearly impossible to draw from an ankle holster while moving. Some people also find the weight of an ankle holster on a single leg somewhat disconcerting and hard to get used to.

Day Planner

There are many kinds of holsters of this type. Basically this is a holster concealed within another device. Briefcases, purses, backpacks, and yes, day planners, all can have a hidden compartment to hold a firearm. These are all very comfortable, as the weapon is carried off the body; however, it is easy to lose the holster and, with it, the handgun. Care must be taken not to set it down without constant supervision.

Figure 7.10
Day Planner

Fanny Pack

Fanny packs were once good concealment, but then rapidly became synonymous with concealed carry. At one time, anyone carrying a fanny pack was thought to also be carrying a handgun. This belief has been reduced slightly, but it is still prevalent. If you can get past this perception, fanny packs do offer great concealment.

Figure 7.11
Fanny Pack

A problem with many of these holsters, especially crossdraw, shoulder, and fanny pack holsters, is muzzling by standards during draw. Muzzling is the process of unintentionally pointing the muzzle of a firearm in an unsafe direction. This is also called "lasering," meaning that if you imagined a laser that was always on coming out of your barrel that anything in the path of this imaginary laser was cut. Whatever you call it, you need to be sure that your firearm is always pointed at a safe direction even while it's moving.

First Experiences Carrying Concealed

When you first begin to carry a handgun it is common to feel very conspicuous. You may feel that everyone is looking at you or that your handgun is obvious. Your body language will probably do more to point out the fact that you are armed than the gun does. You are liable to be stiff or unconsciously check to see if the gun is still where you put it.

As time goes by this feeling of conspicuousness will go away. You will probably never get so comfortable that you forget you are armed, and you shouldn't. Time will make you more comfortable, and that comfort will make your concealment that much more effective.

To ensure your comfort, and to make that steep learning curve a little easier, I recommend wearing your chosen holster/firearm combination around your home a few days just to "break it in." By doing so, you will learn what movements will make your handgun "print" or outline against your clothes, and how carrying the handgun actually feels.

Chapter 9

Shooting Techniques

Certain basic techniques must be mastered if one is to progress from simply firing a firearm to one who can shoot.

Difference Between the Range and the Street

One must be careful to differentiate between the range and the street. What works great on the level clean floors of a range, in the well-lit atmosphere, with the big non-moving paper targets, and the low-stress environment might not work in a dark, crowded alleyway. Let us not forget the adrenaline effects, stress, time constraints, or the little added bonus of *someone shooting at us*!

Practice your skill in a realistic manner; be honest with yourself. Do not cheat yourself by taking shortcuts. It is a well-established fact that, in a stressful situation, you will revert to the level of training that you have mastered and not perform at your best.

Learn to shoot, shoot consistently into groups, and then troubleshoot your actions to move those groups on the paper. If you take the shortcut of "Kentucky Windage" you will not be able to perform on the street. What I mean is that if you always shoot low and left, aiming high and right only works using paper targets. In a real situation, you will not have a fixed aiming point. Would you want to explain in court that you were actually aiming at some imaginary point not on the body of your attacker when answering questions as to why you missed and hit an innocent bystander? Any instructor worth the time you are spending with him or her should never tell you to fix your aiming errors by "aiming off." It's just lazy, and will cause you more problems in the long run.

Gripping the Handgun

Obviously the first movement is to establish a proper grip on the pistol. The correct shooting grip must start in the holster. A proper grip begins with the pistol grip being placed into the "V" formed between the thumb and index finger of the dominant hand. The higher your hand is on the pistol, the more recoil will be absorbed by your grip. Ideally, the barrel will be in line with the forearm.

To illustrate why, get an unloaded firearm and hold the pistol grip so that the hand is as low on the grip as possible. The barrel should be high above the top of your hand. With your support hand rock the pistol up and down to simulate recoil. Now, drop the pistol deeper into your hand and simulate recoil again. You should notice that the lower the handgun sits in your hand, the better you can control its recoil motion.

A strong, consistent grip on the handgun should be maintained. A strong, consistent grip is not a death grip. When using a two-handed grip, the dominant hand should grip the pistol with the same intensity as a firm handshake. Too strong of a grip will not only cause the handgun to shake, it will make it impossible to manipulate the trigger rapidly and smoothly. If you notice that you have to reestablish your grip after each shot, you are not gripping the handgun hard enough.

Whenever possible, one should use a two-handed grip. A two-handed grip allows for the best control of the firearm. To perform a two-handed grip, begin with the dominant hand gripping the pistol as above, then place the heel of the support hand palm on the exposed grip, just forward of the dominant hand palm, and just behind the tips of the dominant hand fingers. Wrap your support hand fingers around the dominant hand, so that the top of the support hand index finger presses against the bottom of the trigger guard. The more skin the shooter can place on the handgun, the more control he or she has on the firearm.

The support hand should provide 80% of the grip strength. This tight, strong grip will reduce felt recoil. It will do this better than a tight grip by the strong hand because it will not involve the trigger finger, freeing the trigger finger to move unencumbered.

For the most part, I don't create a distinction between different types or models of firearms. After all, fundamentals of shooting are fundamental. One thing that is different between revolvers and semi-automatics is where you place your thumb. If you are firing a revolver, you need to place your thumb over the top of your firing hand. This keeps it away from the cylinder of the revolver so that gasses escaping from the front of the cylinder do not burn you or spatter you with lead shavings.

If you fire a semi-automatic with your thumb over your firing hand, you will experience what I call a "self-correcting error."

With a semi-automatic the thumbs should be placed so that the support thumb is underneath the strong thumb. The dominant thumb locks it in place so it does not get bit by the recoiling slide. The tip of each thumb is pointing toward the target. If the thumbs are allowed to point up, they can inadvertently press against the slide, retarding its movement and causing malfunctions.

Figure 9.01
2-handed Grip

Make sure that the thumbs are against the frame and not touching the slide of a semi-automatic. The thumbs should neither accidentally press up or down on the slide lock of a semi-auto, nor accidentally release the magazine on a semi-automatic.

Self-Correcting Error

No matter what I try, every class I have includes a student with a semi-automatic who refuses to hold the pistol in the correct manner. The student feels more comfortable with his or her support thumb riding on the top of the dominant hand right below and behind the slide. I explain in detail what will happen, and continually tell the student to change his or her grip on the range. I even joke that the student will soon see why this is a self-correcting error. This student ends the class with a band-aid on the knuckle of his or her thumb, because the slide recoils back and slices the thumb open.

Figure 9.02
Proper Thumb Placement is
Important to Avoid Injury

This is not said to downgrade my students; it is my fault as an instructor for not stopping this from happening. But invariably, when the range lesson is over, my students tell me that this is a self-correcting error, because they "sure ain't gonna do it again!" Please learn from this and see that proper techniques have a reason behind them and, until you know the reasons why something is done a certain way, do it correctly.

I drill into my students that you cannot begin to think outside the box until you understand the parameters of the box, why the box is there, and why it's a box and not a bag. There are times when you can adjust and throw technique out the window. But it takes some time to know when that's appropriate.

Drawing the Gun

Having a gun on your person and possessing the ability to hit what you are aiming at will not serve you very well if you are not able to draw your firearm from its holster and get it into service. There is a lot of misinformation floating around about gunfighting, especially gunfighting in the American West. The gunfighters of the 1800s were not so much quick draw artists as men who were able to stand up to the pressure of lethal encounters.

Too often, shooters can rush into attempting to build speed before they are smooth and competent in performing the necessary movements at normal speed. This causes a hit-or-miss, jerky draw that is fumbled as often as it is fast. This is not consistent with proper training. Preparation for a lethal force encounter should create the ability to perform on demand no matter what the circumstances.

Always train using the techniques you will use on the street. Start slowly, and practice perfect movements. When you practice incorrect movements, you will ingrain these incorrect movements in your mind. If this happens you will perform these incorrect movements when proper functioning matters.

By using the term incorrect movements, I am describing movements that contain extra actions, or that are not stress resistant. Current firearm techniques are the products of a hundred years of combat distillation; any movements that are not needed have been stripped away.

Practice these movements to be as smooth as possible. Smooth movements are fast; jerky attempts at speed are slow.

Above all, once you understand the movements and how to perform them correctly, you must practice them continuously. Bruce Lee once stated that he was not afraid of the man that practiced 10,000 kicks once, but he was afraid of the man that practiced one kick 10,000 times.

Shooting is a lot like riding a bike—once you have ingrained the movements you won't forget. But just because you know how, doesn't mean you will stay at your top level of mastery. If you haven't ridden your bike since your were 10 years old, do you think you are ready to go mountain biking without a refresher? Shooting is a degradable skill just like any other skill. Once you learn it, you must continue to practice to keep at your top performance.

Drawing the Handgun from the Dominant Side

The following techniques form the established method for drawing the handgun from the dominant side. This is the most common method, and portions such as grip and support-hand placement translate to other methods for drawing from other holster types.

As stated previously, the proper grip should be established while the gun is still in the holster. As you decide to draw, reach down with your dominant hand and establish a proper grip on your handgun. It may be necessary to use your dominant side thumb to rake back any covering garment, or use your support hand to rip the tail of your shirt upward if you are wearing an inside-the-waistband holster. If the support hand is not needed to help clear garments or fight off attack, it should be

Figure 9.03
Grip is established while the gun is in the holster, and the support hand is brought into the body

brought toward the centerline of the body. I personally place my support hand in the center of my stomach directly underneath my ribs. Doing this simultaneously with the strong hand gripping the handgun keeps the support hand out of the way, and allows it to be in place for a later step in the draw.

Once the grip is established, the handgun should be drawn from the holster and rotated forward so that the upper arm is along the body line (your upper arm should be along your side) and the forearm is parallel to the ground. Keep the handgun safety on and the finger off the trigger at this point.

The last and final step in the three-step draw is to bring the handgun forward into firing position. As the handgun moves, the support hand should move to intercept and grasp the handgun. Ensure that the support hand moves in from the side of the handgun and not in front of the muzzle. The support hand should be brought to the handgun, not the handgun being brought to the support hand. Remember, nothing should cross the muzzle of your gun that you are not willing to shoot.

Practice each step alone until the moves are smooth and consistent. Bring them together slowly. Do not rush to add speed. Speed will come on its own as your skill level increases.

Figure 9.04
Rock the gun out of the holster with forearm parallel to ground

Figure 9.05
While pushing the gun out toward your shooting stance, bring your support hand up to meet it. Watch the muzzle!

Figure 9.06
The draw stroke is completed when you are in your proper shooting stance.

Reholster

Firearm expert Massad Ayoob says that the mark of a master pistolero is the ability to holster a gun without looking at the holster. Reholstering is an important skill, as you want to put the handgun back without it snagging on the holster, or having the muzzle cross your body. This is important, but it is also important to remember that speed is not an issue in reholstering.

ALWAYS REHOLSTER RELUCTANTLY.

Never reholster your firearm if you still feel threatened.

Once the threat is over (and any safety devices are activated), bring the rear of the handgun to your chest, and scan left and right to look for additional threats. Bureau of Justice Crime studies have suggested that, for the average armed robbery, four additional accomplices are present that do not show themselves to the victim. The time to notice these additional street rats is while your handgun is out and you are aware, not when you have let down your guard.

After you have scanned the area, remove your support hand from the handgun and place it at your centerline, bring the handgun down with your strong hand, and angle the muzzle into the holster from the rear of the holster. As you slide the handgun into the holster, keep your trigger finger straight and off the trigger as always, except now this position has an additional reason other than just safety. Use the trigger finger to push any retention straps out of the way and to protect the trigger guard from having any objects slide inside it and snag on the trigger as you holster the firearm.

Lastly, use your strong hand to fasten any retention straps or snaps that are present on your holster.

Fundamentals of Marksmanship

Shooting a firearm is an athletic skill; it is physical and takes practice. Like other skills, there is a body of research into the easiest methods to achieve proficiency. There are certain fundamentals that, if understood and followed competently, enhance your ability to hit your target. If these fundamentals are not mastered prior to the stress of a lethal force encounter, it is unlikely that your rounds will go where you intend them to go. Remember that shot placement is the key to successfully ending a lethal force situation.

Stance

As with all martial arts, balance is the foundation of proper shooting fundamentals. Proper stance allows balance, movement, and stability. This might not be as important at a firing range shooting at stationary targets, but proper stance is crucial on the street. Bull's-eyes don't shoot back, but bad guys do, and let me assure you, you will be much more comfortable if you can move toward cover while firing rather than standing still just like on the range. A proper stance allows this.

Weaver

Of the two primary stances, the weaver is the oldest. It is named for its creator, police officer Jack Weaver. Officer Weaver created this position to win a popular shooting contest held by shooting icon Colonel Jeff Cooper. In this quick-draw competition, the shooters lined up on the firing line seven yards from the targets. The contest was simple, just draw and shoot. At that time, the preferred shooting method was called point shooting; the shooter fired one handed from the hip just like a TV cowboy. It looks good, and it was very fast. The problem was that when everyone's guns were empty and the smoke cleared nobody ever hit their targets. Deputy Weaver decided that a pretty quick hit beat a lightning fast miss. Shortly after he won the competition, everyone was using the two-handed Weaver stance and aiming their shots.

Figure 9.07
Weaver Stance

The Weaver is most commonly seen on TV. It begins with a boxer's stance, or what is known in law enforcement circles as an interview stance. This means that the body is partly sideways in relation to the target rather than "squared off" facing it. Both hands are on the firearm, holding it at eye level. Both elbows are flexed, with the strong side elbow slightly bent, and the support side elbow flexed almost 90 degrees. The arms perform a "push-pull" that creates muscular tension. The strong arm pushes the gun toward the target, while the support arm pulls it toward the body. This tension is the main aspect of the Weaver.

This stance was very popular with law enforcement, as it was perceived as presenting less of a target to hostile fire because the body is bladed (sideways). It is also simple for law officers to use because the position is based on the stance used to speak with suspects. It has been my experience that first-time shooters naturally assume a variation of the Weaver stance without prompting. When asked, they normally state that it feels natural. I believe that stems from the popularity of this stance in movies.

Some problems with the Weaver are that it relies on muscular strength to maintain tension, and it can also be complicated to use because of the different amounts of tension and the different elbow positions.

There are many variations of this stance. I particularly like the Chapman version. In this stance, created by Ray Chapman, the strong side elbow is locked, and the strong arm is straight. This creates a bone on bone lock, and removes some of the problems inherent to the basic Weaver.

Isosceles

This stance is much simpler than the Weaver. It begins by directly facing the target with your legs shoulder width apart. The knees are slightly bent. The handgun is punched straight out from the center of your chest with both arms fully extended. This will place the firearm in a position that is centered on your body. In essence, you are aiming the firearm with your body. Your upper body should lean slightly forward.

While it may seem more natural to lean backward, this places you off balance. To demonstrate, get into an isosceles stance without a handgun, lean back and then try to move to the side. It is almost impossible to do so. Try it again while leaning forward. It is

Figure 9.08
Isosceles Stance

much easier to move to the side when leaning forward. In a real-life situation where you are going to want to be moving, you should use a stance that allows movement.

I prefer the Isosceles; I began to study it after reading Andy Stanford's book *Surgical Speed Shooting*. I learned that this stance is used almost exclusively by national champions competing in both the IDPA and IPSC (defensive shooting competitions). These competitions are extremely competitive and speed driven. After practicing on my own and applying the techniques both in competition and at the range, I have become a fan of this technique and use it as my primary stance.

I was further impressed when I learned that videos of gunfights recorded on police cruiser cameras showed that, while policemen might begin a gunfight shooting with a Weaver stance, they unconsciously and rapidly transitioned to the Isosceles. This is thought to be due to the way the body processes information. Because the body receives almost 80% of its information visually, and the eyes are centered on the body, in a gunfight the mind reflexively centers the body on the target to get more information.

If you need more proof that the body instinctively squares itself toward the threat, give someone permission to scare you at some unexpected time. Do you blade your body to the threat, or do you squarely face it?

Having a favorite stance or a favorite gun is great, but it is still important to be knowledgeable about multiple stances and using multiple techniques. Every skill you possess is one more tool in your toolbox, something that you can fall back on if your "go-to" position fails to provide the desired results.

Sight Alignment

Sight alignment is one of the fundamentals of shooting. Sight alignment is the positioning of the gun so that the eye aligns with the rear sight in such a way that the front sight is even and centered with the rear sight, and the sights appear to be superimposed on the target.

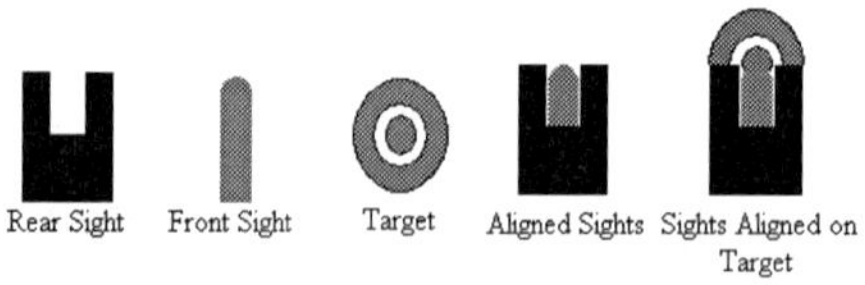

Sight alignment is what allows you to shoot accurately. If the sights are aligned on the target at the instant the handgun is fired, then the round will land where you told it to go. If the sights are not

Rear Sight   Front Sight   Target   Aligned Sights   Sights Aligned on Target

Figure 9.09
Sight Alignment

aligned on the target, then the round will head where the sights were aligned. Rounds do not miss; they always hit something. Always ensure that you aim at what you wish to hit.

The human eye can focus only at one distance at a time. If a photographer takes a picture of a butterfly in the foreground, a family, and a far-off mountain as a backdrop, two items are going to be out of focus.

It is impossible to focus on the rear sight, the front sight, and the target at the same time. This is not as large a problem as it seems. Sight alignment is lining up the front sight in the center of the rear sight, and then placing those sights on the target. To do this, you only need to focus on the front sight. If you do this, you will still be able to see the rear sight and the target. They might be blurry, but you will be able to make them out. Train out the temptation to look at the target. If you look at the target you will not be able to even see the rear sight.

Figure 9.10 and Figure 9.11
Focus on the FRONT SIGHT. Everything But the Front Sight is Blurry, Just as It Should Be.

Flash Sight Picture

If you have the fundamentals down, and you are practicing for self-defense, you can gauge your progress with a 9-inch paper plate or a sheet of typing paper. As long as your hits are on this target you are doing fine. If your hits can be covered with your hand, you are shooting too slowly. Speed up. While you cannot shoot fast enough if you are not hitting your target, shooting too slowly is a problem if it gets you killed.

To shoot quicker at short distances (3 – 7 yards) the flash sight picture is used. Flash sight picture is a function of shooting for speed, as differentiated from shooting for accuracy. As discussed earlier, the statistical gunfight is a close affair. Surgical accuracy is not needed.

When using the flash sight picture, if you can see your rear sight, the front sight is somewhere inside the rear sight, and the front sight is centered on the target, you can shoot. At short distances, the sights do not have to be precisely aligned to hit center mass of a human-sized target.

Flash sight picture does not replace fundamentals, and it requires practice, but it is much faster then a precisely aimed shot. Flash sight picture is *still aiming*; this is not permission to fire blindly. You must always use your sights. And as always you are still responsible for your bullets.

This is a balancing act of speed versus accuracy. The farther your target is away from you, the more likely that a flash sight picture will cause you to completely miss your target. But taking time to minutely adjust your sights while some human cockroach is stabbing you surely isn't fast enough.

Trigger Pull

Trigger pull is another fundamental technique a person must learn to ensure consistent hits on target. Trigger pull allows the shooter to ignite the firing sequence of the cartridge without disturbing proper sight alignment.

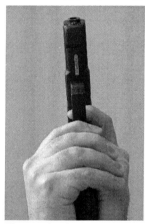

Proper trigger pull is not like it sounds. The trigger must not be pulled. It should not be jerked. The trigger must be squeezed. I prefer to use the term trigger press. The word press conjures a mental image of a single finger pressing a button, but the word pull makes me think of a man using his whole body to pull on a rope. You should take care to only use your trigger finger to manipulate the trigger. A common error is to squeeze the entire hand slightly causing the firearm to shift.

Figure 9.12 Proper Finger Placement on the Trigger Helps Control the Handgun.

Once mastered, it is not necessary to slowly squeeze the trigger. This operation can be done with speed. The essential element is that the trigger must be manipulated smoothly, without jerking. The trigger should break cleanly, firing the ammunition without the shooter being consciously aware that the gun will fire.

When you're talking to people about how to shoot a gun, sooner or later you are going to hear that if you're properly squeezing the trigger it should be a surprise when the gun actually discharges. That's true, but only if you think about it in a particular way. If you have only learned one thing so far, I hope that it's the fact that you are responsible for every shot that you fire. It is hard to take responsibility for surprises. It is not that the gun should surprise you; it's that you should not anticipate the recoil

Anticipating the round firing causes you to flinch. Flinching leads to jerking the gun. Jerking the gun, in turn, changes the sight picture. This causes the round to impact off target.

Anticipating the gun going off is primarily caused by your internal self-talk. You know the little voice in your head that tells you what to do, and *when* to do it. You want to smoothly and continually press the trigger rearward until the firearm discharges rather than line up the sights and have your self-talk cause you to pull the trigger right *now*. If you smoothly press the trigger without a mental *now*, then you will have achieved a "surprise" break because you did not know the exact millisecond the firearm went off.

One test to see if you are jerking the trigger is called the ball and dummy exercise. In this exercise have a partner load your handgun. Have them place one round (either live or a special non-firing dummy round) in the handgun. Your partner then places the pistol in your holster. You draw and fire. If you get a dummy round you will notice your flinch because there will be no recoil to cover it.

Breath Control

Breath control is also a basic mechanical skill needed when firing a gun. Breathing causes the chest to rise and affects the shooter's natural point of aim. This changes the sight alignment. Because breathing is an essential involuntary action, it cannot be stopped. Therefore, it must be controlled.

To control your breathing, you may take advantage of the natural respiratory pause. Take a second to breathe, notice that there is a small pause after you both exhale and inhale. This is a controllable, repeatable event that is the perfect time to fire a shot.

Another widely used technique to control breathing is the Figure 8. Although the Figure 8 is mostly practiced with rifles, it does have utility with handguns if practiced. It is done by slightly and imperceptibly moving the gun in a figure eight pattern while inhaling and exhaling. If done correctly your natural respiratory pause will occur when the firearm is in the meeting point of the two circles. You should begin taking up the slack in the trigger while moving toward the center and with practice you can fire the handgun while in the center of the imaginary figure eight. This causes the gun to be fired at the same point each time.

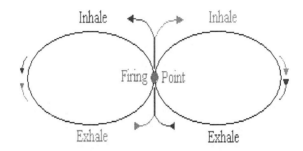

Figure 9.13
Figure 8 Breathing Method

Follow-through

The last fundamental of marksmanship is follow-through. Follow-through is simply continuing with the fundamentals after the shot and then reacquiring the target. You decide to shoot; you draw, aim, and squeeze a round out; then, as soon as the recoil stops, you immediately acquire a new sight picture. This is follow-through. You must always acquire one more sight picture than rounds fired. If you fire only once, then you must look through your sights at the target twice—once before, and once after.

Follow-though in combat allows you to ask the following questions and then answer with another round if necessary.

Did I hit my target? You should know where your round went because you were looking at the sight picture when the gun went off. Following through will force better concentration on the fundamentals. Did my target go down? Was your shot enough, or are you still being threatened? If you train yourself to automatically prepare a follow-up shot, you will be vastly quicker with that shot if needed. Remember: Don't put the weapon down until the threat is over.

Proper follow-through also helps with training as it makes you think about what you are doing and allows you to spot some of your mistakes so you can correct them, but its most important purpose is that it aids accuracy. Follow-through keeps you from imperceptibly moving the gun in the split second the bullet is moving down the barrel.

Common Errors

There are some errors common to both experienced and inexperienced shooters. Although no book can take the place of competent instruction, information on these common errors can help the new shooter.

Reading the Target

It is a common practice, albeit a poor one, to worry about the target while practicing. While shooting on the range, do not attempt to see where your rounds are impacting on the target while firing. Think internally, worry about what you are doing. Ensure that during practice you are making correct movements, applying the fundamentals, and, above all, being consistent.

One of the things I like best about firearms is that it is more a mental than physical sport. Firearms are a great equalizer. As far as accuracy is concerned what's going on internally with your head and body is more important than external factors like weather and time of day. If you get too concerned with your target you may start to have negative self-talk. I have noticed that when my students start shaking their head and saying "ah man" after a dropped shot, their next shot isn't all that good either. Keep your talk positive. Tell yourself what you *should* do, not what you shouldn't. Instead of "Don't jerk the trigger" tell yourself to "slowly press the trigger rearward until you feel the gun discharge."

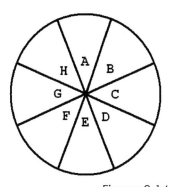

Figure 9.14
Octant Error
Analysis Chart

Once you are shooting consistently, you begin to create groups of holes in your target. It is these groups that allow you to diagnose errors. When you are doing the same things over and over, you can begin to fix your problems. When you are "chasing the bull's-eye" by trying something new every round because you

are watching the target for each shot, you will never know what
your real problems are.

If you use the following list with figure 9.11 you can diagnose
common errors to see what you can do to help put your rounds
into the black of the bulls-eye. This chart is for right-handed
shooters; if you are left-handed, simply reverse the chart.

- **A** — Breaking Wrist Up — If the wrist is unlocked, the
  handgun is allowed to move upward causing the rounds to
  impact high on the target.

- **B** — Heeling Anticipating Recoil — This is applying
  pressure with the strong side heel of the hand, pushing
  the handgun up and to the right.

- **C** — Thumbing — Too much pressure applied to the side
  of the pistol with the thumb; it forces the handgun to the
  right.

- **D** — Tightening Grip While Pulling Up on Trigger —
  The grip should not be changed while shooting. Squeezing
  the grip of the handgun while firing a round will cause the
  front sight of the pistol to move.

- **E** — Breaking Wrist Down or Dropping Head — Trying to
  compensate for recoil or otherwise pressing your wrist
  down, or dropping your head and changing your sight
  alignment will cause the rounds to impact low on the
  target.

- **F** — Jerking or Tightening Fingers — Tightening the
  fingers will push the grip of the handgun into your palm;
  this will force the barrel to be aimed toward the left.

- **G** — Trigger Finger Not Placed Correctly on Trigger —
  Improper trigger finger placement can push the trigger,
  and the handgun, to the left.

- **H** — Pushing: Anticipating Recoil — This is similar to B,
  Heeling. Instead of pushing with the heel of your hand,
  the pushing is done with the wrist. This moves the
  handgun upwards and to the left.

Fatigue

Firearm shooting is called a sport for a reason. Firing a handgun is an athletic sport. As a matter of fact, President Jefferson stated that shooting should be the primary sport for the development of both the mind and the spirit of Americans.

It is not uncommon for a new shooter's accuracy to falter toward the end of a 50-round box of ammunition. This is not only due to the physical stress of holding a piece of steel out from your body, but it is also a factor of the extreme mental concentration needed to successfully fire a handgun.

Jerking the Trigger

A very common error is for the shooter to jerk the trigger instead of smoothly pressing it rearward. This can be caused by poor muscular control, nervousness caused by the handgun firing, bad habit, or ignorance. Whatever the reason, the effect is the same. Jerking the trigger causes the shot to go somewhere other than your intended destination.

We talked earlier about the ball and dummy drill, and how it will allow you to see if you jerk the trigger or have a noticeable flinch. You can also place an empty shell or a coin along the top of the frame of an unloaded firearm. If you attempt to fire and you jerk the trigger, the object will likely fall off.

There is an exercise that will help teach your finger how to squeeze smoothly without jerking or using the entire hand. Fill a turkey baster with water; hold it in your dominant hand. Use your trigger finger to squeeze only one drop at a time into a bowl. Once you get this down, you will be able to let a drop hang on the tip and drop at the exact moment you desire.

Chapter 10

Tactics

You Perform as You Train

I commonly see or hear students who think that once they take a class and apply for a permit they no longer need any practice or additional training. This can cause problems, especially when adult learning theory states that the average adult retains only 25% of course information two weeks after the class ends.

Add to this lack of retention the extreme stress of a lethal force situation and the physical nature of gun handling, and it becomes apparent that practice is a vital part of preparedness. You will not rise to the challenge of a gunfight. You will default to your proven abilities. If you cannot shoot consistent 9-inch groups at 15 yards on the range, what makes you think you can do it in the low-light, stressful, fast, rapidly evolving arena of a gunfight? Practice your skills, but more important than that, practice your skills perfectly. Ingrain in your mind a groove that you can unconsciously slide into when the lead stuff is coming at the red stuff. Practice often so that you do not have to think about your actions.

Movement

In the Marine Corps, a fighting vehicle had to be able to do three things to be considered "live." It had to be able to shoot, to move, and to communicate. We covered shooting in Chapter 9 and communication in Chapter 5; now we are briefly going to cover movement.

Besides the live person shooting back at you, and the stress placed on you, movement is the biggest difference between being on the range and on the street. It is also something that you can practice. I used to be amazed at videos showing instructors moving while shooting from the Isosceles position. Once I tried it at a shooting school I learned that, once you have a stable position to shoot from and have the fundamentals down, it is not really all that hard. If you get into a gunfight, be prepared to make aggressive movements. Move to cover; get something in front of you that can stop bullets, not just conceal you from your attacker's view.

If you want more training in this area I highly recommend trying out action shooting competitions. If you don't get too involved in trying to win that you forget proper tactics, IDPA and other clubs provide you with a cost effective way to get to practice shooting while moving and other tactical skills while having a safety person right behind you.

Cover/Concealment

There is a difference among the objects you can hide behind. The difference is that some things stop sight, and some things stop bullets. Cover is anything that can protect you from incoming rounds. An Abrams M1A1 tank is a good example. If you have a battle tank between you and Mr. Street Rat, it is unlikely that his 9 mm bullets will hurt you.

Concealment, on the other hand, is something that does not stop bullets but hides you from the view or attention of the attacker. A child hidden under a bed is an example of concealment. A dark corner is another example. Darkness can hide you, so it can be good concealment.

Some objects provide cover from some guns and concealment only from others. I was lucky to be on the range training when my old prison warden brought a salesman down to demonstrate some new bullet-resistant glass. Because the glass was to cover my work station, I was naturally interested. The glass could take 6 rounds at point blank range from a .38 and not even dimple. We were impressed; my wonder at this plastic fantastic faltered a little when a single .223 rifle round not only penetrated the glass but did so easily.

You should also be aware that items may have a bullet-soaking lifespan. A wall may take 4 or 5 rounds and protect you, but that 6th round penetrates due to the weakening of the structure. Also of importance, it has been shown that a round impacting on a solid surface (car hoods were used in the experiments) will rise a few inches and travel along the top of the object. If you use your car as cover, get back from it, and stay as low as possible. Although TV stars may use the car hood for support, they also are not being shot at with real bullets.

Low-light

Once again we will talk about statistics. The FBI's uniform crime statistics show that most gunfights occur at times or in areas of reduced lighting. Criminals like the dark. The darkness in no way reduces your requirement of target identification. These statistics make it a good idea to learn how to use a flashlight effectively in conjunction with your sidearm.

There are many methods for using a flashlight along with your firearm. I prefer two of what I consider the simplest methods. The first method is called the Harries. The Harries is the earliest of modern combat flashlight techniques. In this technique, the flashlight is carried as a club. The bulb end of the flashlight is held in the support hand near the pinkie finger. The flashlight is then passed under the dominant hand so that the palms meet. This technique can become tiring over time, and it does not give a lot of support to the firing hand.

I also like the Surefire/Rodgers technique. The main drawback to this technique is that it requires a small flashlight with a push-button switch on the tail cap. In this method the flashlight is held between the middle two fingers of the support hand, with the tail switch pressed against the heel of the palm. This allows the support hand to be used in a conventional two-handed grip of the pistol. It also allows the light to be turned on by squeezing the support hand.

No matter the technique used, do not keep the light on constantly. Turn it on, identify the threat, fire, and turn it off. The light gives your location away.

It is especially important to keep a light near your bedside gun so that you have a ready source of light inside your home.

Examples of Flashlight Techniques

Figure 10.01
Harries Method

Figure 10.02
Surefire/Rodgers

Retention

I read quite a bit of anti-gun press, which seems stuck on the notion that people should not carry a gun because it can be taken away from the armed citizen and used against him or her. This assumes the citizen will allow the gun to be taken away. While it is possible for a handgun to be wrestled away from the owner, ask yourself a question. Would you attempt to take a handgun away from someone you believed would shoot you if you tried?

While your attitude may reduce the likelihood of a criminal trying to disarm you, your posture can help you physically retain your handgun. When you open a new jar of pickles, do you hold the jar out from your body in a good isosceles stance? Or do you bring the jar close into your body to use your weight to its full advantage? It is the same for handgun retention. Although a good Isosceles or Weaver stance works well for shooting, these stances do not work well at contact distances because they allow the criminal to get closer to your weapon than you can.

One good weapon retention position keeps the handgun tucked into the strong side of the body. The handgun should be slightly angled, and the slide should be held away from the body with the grip held near the body. This keeps the slide on an automatic from catching in your shirttail, or having its movement retarded by your body. This will prevent misfires. The support hand should be up and held in a blocking position. This may sound obvious, but if someone is attempting to disarm you, you are in a physical fight; use all the options, punches, slaps, gouges, and rounds from the handgun. Use any method to get your attacker off and away from you. This is worth practicing on the range; however, in a training situation, keep your support hand on your chest, with your support elbow tucked into your body and be very careful about the angle of the gun. You do not want

Figure 10.03
Hip Retention Position

any part of your body or another person's in front of the muzzle during training.

Tactical Pyramid

Temperament and training trump tools and tactics. When I was a child my parents bought a piano. Having access to it did not make me a concert musician; neither did the guitar, clarinet, or drum lessons they paid for. I refused to practice, so I never became competent. Owning a gun does not make you skilled in its use. Guns are tools. You have to learn to use them.

The will is more important than the skill. And the skill is more important than the actual handgun you use.

The mindset that you will not be a victim is the most important combative tool you can have. Add to that proper training and practice to hone your instincts and abilities. Once you have those two essentials in place you may worry about specific tactics to use in actual situations. If you have these three things in place, you are ready no matter if you are armed with a $50 used revolver or a $2,000 custom combat competition handgun.

I am sure that every master carpenter who builds homes has a favorite hammer. But I am equally sure he would still be able to build a home if he had to use someone else's hammer. Firearms are tools, and it's the skill and knowledge that make them work, not the tool alone.

Figure 10.04
Start at the Base and Work Upward

Chapter 11

Common Myths

Shoot and Drag

If you shoot a burglar and then drag him inside your home, you will likely go to prison. Legal use of lethal force requires the ability for your attacker to kill you at that exact moment, and the belief that your attacker is going to kill you. Generally speaking, if you have the right to be at the location you are in, and you have no options to flee (some states do not have a requirement that you first attempt to leave; please consult the laws of your state), you may legally employ deadly force against someone who has the means to kill you and whom you believe is trying to kill you.

If you meet these criteria, the criminal being outside your home or inside should not matter. If he is not a threat, do not shoot him! Anytime you attempt to change the scene, it is going to be assumed that you were in the wrong.

One Shot Stops

There is a video circulating the Internet showing an angry litigant shooting a revolver at a lawyer. The lawyer is ducking back and forth around a tree, while this nut job is shooting him. The criminal finally walks away, and the lawyer raises his hands in a questioning motion and also walks away.

This lawyer was hit several times. The bullets did not "knock him backwards" as they tend to do in movies, nor did a single bullet kill him. This person sustained multiple point blank hits and walked away. This is common.

Handguns are not the most effective means of killing; they are a compromise between portability, concealability, and firepower. If you do not die immediately after being shot, you stand a very good chance of surviving. Never give up, and always keep fighting. Be a survivor and not a victim.

On the other side of the coin, a handgun bullet causes damage based on its size, speed, and shape. This is magnified or reduced based on where the round impacts on the body. There have been extensive studies by the FBI, U.S. military, and private individuals to find the best combinations to effect the miracle "one shot stop." What has been found is that shot placement into the center mass is the most effective means, and if the first round does not cause the desired effect, multiple additional rounds may need to be fired to cause internal bleeding. Do not be discouraged if it takes more than one shot to save your life from an attacker, but only use the amount of shots necessary to neutralize the threat.

That being said, what do you do when someone is trying to kill you and firing a round into him did not stop him? Well, besides uttering an expletive or two, the next section will discuss options.

Mozambique Drill (2 to the Chest, 1 to the Head)

This drill is also named the failure to stop drill. It comes from a story told to Col. Cooper by one of his students. This student was leaving Mozambique under some stressful and dangerous circumstances and was challenged by a man carrying an AK-47. The student drew his pistol and shot the man in the chest twice. These rounds did not seem to have an effect, so he shot the AK-47–bearing attacker in the head with an additional well-aimed shot.

Once this story came out, it became the center of the well meaning but uninformed gun culture. I have heard new students in my courses state that they are not worried about being attacked; if they are attacked, they will simply "put 2 in the chest and one in the head." Real life does not work this way. Head shots are difficult, and hard to manage in the best of situations. The belief that this method will work every time also ignores its realities.

The attacker was wearing body armor, and a head shot was necessary, but this was determined on scene as part of the Observe, Orientate, Decide, and Act (OODA) process. The shooter observed that the attacker absorbed two large caliber handgun hits to the chest; he orientated to the situation by realizing that the attacker was wearing armor. Then he decided the best way to stop the attack was a head shot. The action is obvious; he aimed at the head and ended the attack.

This was not automatic. It was deliberate and based on the situation, as any rounds fired should be. If you must subscribe to this two-to-the-chest mentality, a viable option can be found in *Tactical Pistol Marksmanship: How to Improve Your Combat Shooting Skills* by Gabriel Suarez. In his book, Suarez describes the Mozambique drill and says that, after the first two shots, the sights should automatically be placed at the attacker's head. If the head is seen and the attacker has not been neutralized, a head shot should be fired. I disagree; as at this beginning level, a head shot is a tall order to complete. A way to duplicate the difficulty of a head shot is to blow up a 9-inch balloon and tie it loosely to a target stand on a windy day. If you can hit this moving, unpredictable, and small target, on command, every time, then you can begin to think about being qualified for the Mozambique drill.

A better option may be to aim for the pelvis. If the pelvis has been shattered, it will be hard for the attacker to stand up, much less run at you. The pelvis is also much larger than the head, and it is nearer to other areas of the body, so that a miss aimed at the pelvis has the likelihood of striking a leg or the belly rather than missing the attacker completely as would a miss aimed at the head.

Although some trainers disagree with this method (they don't think a pistol shot would break the hip), others swear by it. I have even heard anecdotal evidence of criminals giving up because they thought their victim was trying to emasculate them.

This is an option for you, because you should know that if the first pair of rounds didn't drop your attacker, it is likely to take a few minutes for them to "bleed-out" and some action needs to be taken; move away, shoot them again, something. Remember, once you are attacked and decide to use deadly force, you are committed to action and must never give up until you are safe.

Chapter 12

Dealing with Criticism

Personal preparedness means different things depending on who you are and your situation. To an inhabitant of the Florida Keys, preparedness means having items to outlast a hurricane. To a city dweller, preparedness might be having a can of mace in her purse. To a survivalist, preparedness might mean having a semi-trailer loaded with M14 rifles buried in the back yard. Depending on the situation, any of these definitions might be appropriate.

Personal preparedness is simply knowing what dangers are likely to befall you and taking reasonable precautions to avoid or survive them. In today's world, insurance is a required item. No one laughs at a car owner who buys a full coverage insurance policy for his or her car. As a matter of fact, a driver who fails to insure his or her car is looked upon as irresponsible, sometimes even criminal. The same thing can be said about homeowner's or renter's insurance, life insurance, or health insurance.

Today, people set aside money for retirement in the form of IRAs, 401(k)s, mutual funds, and the like. No one faults them. Why is it then that someone who has a pantry of stored food, candles, a rifle or two, and ammunition is considered crazy or dangerous? Isn't it a logical extension of the doctrine of insurance? After all, insurance is merely a device to lessen the effect a disaster has on your life. If having an extra insurance policy for break-ins is smart, then the idea of someone breaking into your home is assumed to be possible. If it is likely that someone might break into your home, then having a means to protect yourself is justified.

Each year natural disasters occur in the United States. When these occur, the news media rush to the scene. It never fails that they show a relief organization van at the disaster site. Usually there is an interview with someone who is standing in line looking for help. The sight is common—a desperate parent with a hungry child waiting for someone to give him or her some milk for the infant. Ratings soar and people feel sorry for this poor child. Consider that areas prone to natural disasters are known. Floods happen on a regular basis. Places like Tornado Alley have been recognized and named. If the choice is made to live in an area like this and basic precautions are not taken, then pity is not the logical emotion. Irresponsibility on the part of the parent caused the child's pain; it only takes a few extra seconds to grab a couple extra bottles of formula. Why didn't the parents take this simple precaution? They probably paid the cable bill. Does that expense outweigh the measly cost of a gallon of bottled water?

Organizations like the American Red Cross and the Office of Homeland Security suggest that each family have a stock of essential items to get them through a few days in case of an emergency. Doing this is not hard nor does it have to be expensive. No one says that preparedness means having a year's supply of freeze dried steak in a concrete storage bunker. Simply buying an extra can or two of food every time you go shopping is enough. Buy an extra box of garbage bags, some extra toilet tissue, or any item you have to have. Store these items in a box under the bed, or in the closet. In hardly any time at all, you will have a stock pile that will give you not only an added measure of security, but also a sense of well-being. Rotate this stock out. As you eat a box of macaroni, buy another. Forget that you have four boxes on your kitchen shelf. This helps you to not feel over-burdened financially to support your prepared lifestyle. It also keeps your store fresh. An added benefit is that your safety net is familiar to you. In the stressful time of disaster, you don't have the added stressor of eating unfamiliar foods chosen not by your appetite, but by their shelf life.

It is easy to lecture on what items are needed. Lists of essential items depend on lifestyle and location as much as physical needs. It would be irresponsible to dictate what equipment your family would need to survive without knowing you or your situation. You must sit down and decide your family's priorities, and from that list correlate your family's needs.

It is not important what others say or think of you. It is not even recommended to tell your neighbors you find the need to be prepared for life. Does it matter if they think you are crazy for stocking up on additional groceries? Will it matter if your children or spouse suffer because you want to keep in the good graces of the people two doors down?

Family

I used to be called Sgt. Tackleberry by my former mother-in-law. She sure did not like her granddaughter showing her the pink .22 rifle with matching pink earmuffs she got for Christmas.

Life is a lot easier with my new mother-in-law. At the onset of the recent Nashville flood, my new bride was on the phone with her Daddy. He was asking if she had enough water and food, and generally inquiring about her welfare. I swelled with pride when she told me her mother told him to shut up because "Genny lives in a prepared household." You cannot choose your family, but having supportive family sure makes life easier.

Your spouse has a say in your decision to go armed. Your spouse is the only person you really need permission from. But if approached correctly, and with a well thought out plan, you're not likely to encounter too much resistance. If you have a spouse or kids then you have an ultimate responsibility to protect them—no matter your gender.

Coworkers

Luckily I do not have to deal with this. In my primary job I can be armed if directed, and in my secondary job, I teach people how to go armed. My coworkers either are pro-gun or ambivalent. I don't work with any anti-gun coworkers. But I know this is not normally the case. My wife is good at dealing with this. She doesn't bring it up, but when the talk turns to people who carry, she casually mentions that I teach the State's carry permit course.

Her coworkers almost always seem surprised and say something like "but he's so nice" (I don't know why the two are mutually exclusive), and ask her how she feels about this; she smiles and says she thinks it's great because I let her buy any gun she wants. This gets her looks sometimes, but she also gets questions later in private about what it feels like to carry a gun. She is honest, knowledgeable, and does not make it a big deal or force her opinion.

This works for me, as many of her coworkers come to my classes, and in one instance I gave a chemical spray class at her job site. She convinced me that the coworkers forced her to promise to spray me. I found out much too late that that was false.

This acceptance might not always be the case, and my wife always follows the rules. Her current job does not allow weapons on the property, so as a law-abiding citizen she follows those rules.

I would recommend not telling people you carry a gun but, if you choose to, be honest and don't be pushy about your views; many more people desire to carry than do carry.

Antis

There is no need to discuss this. If a person is truly anti-gun, the person will never listen and will never hear your arguments. The only thing that can come from talking guns with a rabidly anti-gun person is to solidify your own position in your own mind. It will also help you work out pro-gun arguments to use with those who will listen.

Another Reason Not to Tell Anyone

To me, this criticism is yet another reason not to let people know you carry a firearm. If they do not know you are armed, then they cannot judge you for being armed. But whatever you choose as your personal path, do not let anyone change your mind. It is your life and your choice, whether you choose to go armed or not. This is the ultimate expression of "pro-choice."

Chapter 13

Additional Training

On Your Own

Training is anything that builds, reinforces, or ingrains skills so that a person may perform those skills on demand. Training can be done alone, with a partner, or in a group. What is important is that the training be done correctly, and that when practicing a skill, the skill should always be done correctly. Just going through the motions or sloppily performing an action will only confuse the brain into believing that the skill is unimportant, or that the incorrect method is actually correct.

There are many methods of training; what is important is that at the beginning levels, the student should learn the movements and the reason for the movements. Later these rules can be broken, but only after you know the reasons for these rules.

For individual training, I am a fan of dry-fire practice. It is free, easy, fast, and can be performed at home. I live an hour from my favorite range, so I do not get to live fire as much as I want. Luckily, a person's brain doesn't really know the difference between dry firing and live firing. Dry firing is firing the handgun without ammunition.

To dry fire your pistol, begin by removing all ammunition from the room. Clear the handgun and physically ensure that it is unloaded. For an additional safety step, a bulletproof vest panel can be purchased to hang on the wall as a target. Whether you use such a panel or not, choose a wall in the home that will stop the round should the handgun actually contain a round. Once these steps are complete, you may practice drawing the gun, your stances, movement with the handgun, and the fundamentals of shooting.

Although most modern firearms are safe to dry fire without any additional steps, handguns were not designed to be fired without ammunition. Because of this, special dummy rounds called snap caps were invented. These rounds are inert, but look exactly the same as a live round in size and shape. They are normally made of clear-colored plastic or solid-colored plastic to distinguish them from live rounds. Using these rounds will extend the life of the firing pin if extensive dry-fire practice is done.

Range

When on the range, do not succumb to the temptation of rapid dumping of rounds in imaginary, Walter Mitty scenarios. Visualization is important, but on the range the emphasis should be on marksmanship fundamentals. Use live fire to verify the progress of live-fire training. If you blindly shoot at the target without a goal, then you are training yourself to be sloppy in your shooting. This can render your dry-fire practice useless instead of enhancing it.

It is best to have a planned course of fire and objectives to meet when you go to the range. Have a goal in mind of what skills you wish to work on, and how you will work on them. This will help keep you focused and allow you to chart your progress.

Bring a training partner to the range; besides the friendly competition, having someone there to critique your actions will help you see what you are doing wrong. I never noticed I had a problem leaning backwards in the Isosceles until a training partner told me. Having a partner for you to critique will also allow you to build your skills. It is a fundamental of modern instructional methodology that you never truly learn a skill until you teach it. Watching your partner for mistakes, and learning how to help your partner fix them, will cement in your mind that particular skill.

Reading

It is not always possible to go to the range every week, and it is not possible for any but the truly dedicated to dry fire every day. It *is* possible for the student to read books on the subject. I know that not everyone likes to read, but if you have struggled this far, I am sure that you can spend a little more time reading some of the classics in the field.

Books on the subject do not have to be technical treatises; there are many entertaining, knowledgeable writers. Literature and fiction books can also help you build the warrior mindset. Your brain will take whatever information you put into it and use it to formulate its actions. If you read books on honor and courage, it will subconsciously show. Any thinking, reading, studying, or training you do in this field will be collated in your brain and turned into action later.

Visualization

I personally believe that this is a key to proper mindset. Visualization of an attack and your actions on being attacked help prepare your mind. The body is naturally hesitant when performing a new task, or when placed in a new situation. This hesitancy is an evolved trait that keeps us out of harm. Unfortunately, in the area of self-defense, this hesitancy to act can get you killed.

Playing common, likely scenarios in your mind are almost the same as actually being there, at least from the brain's point of view. Note that I used the words common and likely. It is not likely that you will use your newfound command killing skills to save the Pope's life from terminator aliens from Pluto. Do not waste your time on junk scenarios. Think about what you would do if attacked in a parking lot, at the ATM, at the gas station. What would you do if you were awakened by a burglar? A good place to find these scenarios is in the magazines provided to members of the NRA. These magazines publish accounts of armed citizens who were attacked; because these attacks actually occurred, you can see common locations emerge over time.

Another valid reason for visualization practice is to improve technique. You might get to fire only 50 rounds at the range once a month, but how many times can you visualize firing your handgun while sitting at the office? If you take 10 seconds to visualize a *perfect* shot, and repeat this 6 times, a couple of times a day, you fire 50 rounds a week in your mind. That is four times the amount of practice without any more cost or trouble.

Choosing an Instructor

Personal protection is serious business; however, it has become a business. There are many schools and many more instructors out there competing for your training dollars. While it is possible to learn from any situation, your personal defense training should be from the best available instructor. The following is a guide on what to look for in an instructor.

The most obvious are qualifications; the instructor should have some formal training from an established organization. This is not to say that someone without formal certifications doesn't know about firearms, just that formal training ensures that instructors know instructional methods and techniques beyond what a recreational shooter might have. Formal qualifications also help with legal defensibility if the student ever has to use their training. If a student was trained to an accepted standard by a certified instructor and follows the training, the student's legal liabilities are lessened. The most recognized firearm instructor qualifications are NRA Civilian and Law Enforcement Instructor, State Police Officer Standards and Training Commission (POST) Firearm Instructor, and FBI Firearm Instructor Certification. These three are the most common, but there are many others.

Instructor personality plays a large part in what you take away from a class. Unfortunately, some people become instructors because they need to feed their egos, not because they want to teach. It is important that before you decide on a course you should call the instructor and listen to what the instructor has to say. An overactive ego is something that is very evident with little contact with the instructor. Is the instructor negative; does he or she bad mouth other instructors or companies? The truly competent will not feel the need to do this. Does the instructor spend too much time attempting to impress you with how much he or she knows? Having an instructor who fills the class with his or her "war stories" might be entertaining, but are you paying for entertainment or information? Drill instructors work well in the military; however, civilian training is not the military.

Does the instructor feel the need to downgrade or degrade your equipment because it's not what the instructor prefers to carry? Some instructors hate guns like Glocks, or think revolvers are the best. Some spend class time talking about personal preference. Handguns are personal choices and should be approached as such. The instructor is not the one that has to use, carry, or depend on the firearm; you are.

What is the layout of the course? Does it meet all the necessary legal requirements? If there is a legal time requirement for a carry permit class, does the course fulfill the requirements? Too often a mandated 8-hour class is cut short; while it is always nice to get out of class early, being shortchanged on training time could cause legal problems if the training is ever used for self-defense.

Can the instructor provide references, or can you talk to former students? How long has the instructor been in business? How long has the instructor been using firearms? How many classes does the instructor take himself? It is a good indication of the instructor's level of commitment to the industry to see how much continuing education he or she takes in a year. One 40-hour course does not make a competent instructor. A lifelong devotion to learning and passing that skill on to others does.

Does the instructor teach in a style you can relate to? Some classes are sport based, and this is fine if your interest is shooting sports. But would tactics based on winning a game be what you wish to learn if you desire real-world defensible tactics? Does the facility match the information the instructor is trying to teach? Facilities are not as important as the instructor; however, if the facility doesn't have a range that can accommodate the students because of factors such as size, layout, or restrictions, can you learn as much as you could at a range where you could practice the skills being taught?

Does the instructor have integrity? How does he or she answer tough questions? Will the instructor make up answers, or will he or she tell you that he or she does not know the answer? Will the instructor find out the answer for you? Does the instructor make unreasonable claims or exaggerate his or her own skills? Can the instructor perform the skills being taught?

Basically, is the instructor competent to teach the material, are you comfortable with the instructor, and are you able to learn from the methods used to teach the material? Some instructors use humor, some are dry and serious. Whatever they do or whatever their training styles make sure you are happy, as it's your life you are training to protect.

Conclusion

This book is designed to be a beginning, an easy way to get acquainted with the basics. It was designed to be pre-reading for my courses, because I have noticed that some new shooters want to have study material in advance so that they are prepared for class. I feel that no book, no matter how cleverly written, can out do range time with a qualified instructor.

Please stay safe and if you decide to carry a handgun for personal protection spend time on the range so that if the time ever comes, you are able to go home unhurt after it's over.

Index

Accidents 24

Act 7

Adrenaline 32

After a shooting 42

Attitude 38

Auditory exclusion 34

Awareness 2

    condition orange 4

    condition red 5

    condition white 3

    condition yellow 4

Breath control 101

    figure 8 101

Bureau of Alcohol, Tobacco, Firearms, and Explosives 17

Bureau of Alcohol, Tobacco, Firearms, and Explosives (BATFE) 18

Buying a gun 16, 51

    ammunition size 54

    length of the barrel 52

    size matters 52

C.A.P.S.

    assist the injured 45

    call the police 44

    place your weapon in a safe location 45

    secure the scene 46

Caliber 55, 62

CAPS 46

Carelessness 22

Carry laws 13

Children and guns 26

Choosing an Instructor 123

Cleaning 77

Cleaning materials 78

Clearing procedures 66

Cover/Concealment 108

Criticism 117

    antis 120

    coworkers 119

   family 119
Deadly force 82
Decide 6
Dexterity, loss of 32
Drawing 92
   from the dominant side 93
Eddie Eagle gun safety rules 27
Errors 103
Fatigue 105
Federal Firearms License (FFL) 18
Federal law 18
Firearms 61
   action 62
   barrel 61
   caliber 62
   cartridge 62
   centerfire primer 62
   frame 61
Flash sight picture 99
Flashlight techniques 109
Flinching 101
Follow-through 102
Graham v. Connor 38
Gripping the handgun 89
Gun ownership laws 13
Gun shoe loop-hole 17
Gun show loop-hole 17
Gunfights 31
Handguns
   other types 59
Hangfire 74
Holster types 82
   ankle 86
   belly band 85
   crossdraw 83
   day planner 87
   fanny pack 87
   groin 86
   inside the waistband (IWB) 84
   outside the waistband (OWB) 82
   pocket 86

shoulder 84
small of the back (SOB) 83
Home defense guns 26
Hysterical blindness 34
Ignorance 23
Impaired thinking 33
Instructor, choosing 123
Isosceles stance 97
Jerking the trigger 105
Leg-shot syndrome 40
Liability 19
Loading procedures 68
Low-light 109
Malfunctions 73, 75
double feed 76
revolvers 75
semi-automatics 75
stovepipe 76
Marksmanship
fundamentals of 95
stance 96
May issue laws 14
Mindset
awareness 2
defensive 2
Misfire 74
Movement 107
Mozambique Drill 114
Myths, common 113
Mozambique drill 114
one shot stops 113
shoot and drag 113
Observe 6
OODA loop 6, 7
Open carry vs. concealed 81
Orientate 6
Preparedness 1
Proper mindset 2
Proper tactics 43
Range 122
Reading 122

Reasonableness 38
Recoil 64
Reholster 94
Responsibility 37
Retention 110
Revolvers 72
    mechanics of 64
Revolvers 55
Safeties 72
Safety rules 21
Semi-automatic pistols 57
    mechanics of 64
Semi-automatics 72, 91
Shall issue 14
Shoot to wound/kill/neutralize 40
Sight alignment 98
Slide lock reload 71
Squib load 74
State carry permits 15
Storage 24
    devices 25
Stress response 32
Tachypsychia 35
Tactical pyramid 111
Tactics 107
Tap – Rack – Assess 75
Training 121
Trigger pull 100
Tueller drill 8
Tunnel vision 34
Unloading procedures 66
Vermont carry 15
Visualization 123
Weaver stance 96

OTHER TITLES OF INTEREST
FROM LOOSELEAF LAW PUBLICATIONS, INC.

Handgun Combatives - *2nd Edition*
by Dave Spaulding

Defensive Living
by Dave Spaulding

Crucial Elements of Police Firearms Training
by Brian R. Johnson

Essential Guide to Handguns
Firearm Instruction for Personal Defense & Protection
by Stephen R. Rementer and Bruce N. Eimer, Ph.D.

Instinct Combat Shooting 3rd Edition
Defensive Handgunning for Police
by Chuck Klein

Deadly Force
*Constitutional Standards, Federal Guidelines and Officer
    Survival*
by John Michael Callahan, Jr.

Developing the Survival Attitude
by Phil L. Duran

Tactical Attitude
Learn from Powerful Real-Life Experiences
by Phil L. Duran and Dennis Nasci

Use of Force
Expert Guidance for Decisive Force Response
by Brian A. Kinnaird

Processing Under *Pressure*
Stress, Memory and Decision-Making in Law Enforcement
by Matthew J. Sharps

METTLE
Mental Toughness Training for Law Enforcement
by Laurence Miller, Ph.D.

Condition to Win
Dynamic Techniques for Performance-Oriented
Mental Conditioning
by Wes Doss

Conflict Resolution for Law Enforcement
Street-Smart Negotiating
by Kyle E. Blanchfield, Thomas A. Blanchfield, and
Peter D. Ladd

Citizens Terrorism Awareness and Survival
by Col. Michael Licata, USAF (Ret.)

The Verbal Judo Way of Leadership
Empowering the Thin Blue Line from the Inside Up
by Dr. George Thompson & Gregory A. Walker

Navigating the Legal Minefields of Private Investigations
A Career-Saving Guide for Private Investigators, Detectives &
Security Police
by Ron Hankin

Real World Search & Seizure
by Matthew J. Medina

No One Trips Over a Mountain
Enhancing Officer Safety by Doing the Little Things Right
by Det. Joseph Petrocelli & Matthew Petrocelli, Ph.D.

(800) 647-5547   www.LooseleafLaw.com